Border Nation

'Powerful'
Nikesh Shukla, editor of *The Good Immigrant*

'An accessible, well-researched and indispensable guide, myth-busting at every turn, and charting not just the origins of these violent realities, but of equal importance, how we can dismantle them'
Joshua Virasami, author of *How To Change It: Make a Difference*

'A powerful indictment of borders and border regimes that lays bare the story of how they emerged, how they exercise a tenacious hold on our imagination, and how they enact lethal violence on so many'
Priyamvada Gopal, Professor of Postcolonial Studies at the University of Cambridge

'Cowan brings the very notion of a border into sharp focus in this meticulous and compassionate manifesto'
Juno Mac, co-author of *Revolting Prostitutes: The Fight For Sex Workers' Rights*

'Passionate and laser sharp, Cowan not only exposes how greed, racism and hypocrisy work over generations to wall people out of Britain but also gives us tools to dig tunnels under those walls'
Professor Bridget Anderson, Director of Migration Mobilities Bristol and Professor of Migration, Mobilities and Citizenship, University of Bristol

Outspoken by Pluto
Series Editor: Neda Tehrani

Platforming underrepresented voices; intervening in important political issues; revealing powerful histories and giving voice to our experiences; Outspoken by Pluto is a book series unlike any other. Unravelling debates on feminism and class, work and borders, unions and climate justice, this series has the answers to the questions you're asking. These are books that dissent.

Also available:

Mask Off
Masculinity Redefined
JJ Bola

Behind Closed Doors
Sex Education Transformed
Natalie Fiennes

Lost in Work
Escaping Capitalism
Amelia Horgan

Feminism, Interrupted
Disrupting Power
Lola Olufemi

Split
Class Divides Uncovered
Ben Tippet

Border Nation

A Story of Migration

Leah Cowan

PLUTO  PRESS

First published 2021 by Pluto Press
345 Archway Road, London N6 5AA

www.plutobooks.com

British Library Cataloguing in Publication Data
A catalogue record for this book is available from the British Library

ISBN 978 0 7453 4107 1   Paperback
ISBN 978 1 7868 0702 1   PDF eBook
ISBN 978 1 7868 0704 5   Kindle eBook
ISBN 978 1 7868 0703 8   EPUB eBook

This book is printed on paper suitable for recycling and made
from fully managed and sustained forest sources. Logging, pulping
and manufacturing processes are expected to conform to the
environmental standards of the country of origin.

Typeset by Stanford DTP Services, Northampton, England

Simultaneously printed in the United Kingdom and United States of
America

To my grandmothers

Contents

Acknowledgements   viii

Introduction: Why break down borders?   1
1. In the shadow of the British Empire   11
2. Whitewashing and the myth of the migrant 'outsider'   21
3. Why should migrants contribute?   42
4. Building borders through headlines and column inches   50
5. Everyday borders and *de facto* border guards   74
6. The violence of detention and deportation   98
7. Big business and the 'profit motive' for borders   111
8. Borderlands of resistance   126
Conclusion: Living beyond borders   141

Acknowledgements

Thank you to the team at Pluto, in particular to Neda, for your precision, patience and enthusiasm, and to my agent Millie for her ongoing guidance.

Thank you to those who have encouraged me to keep writing. My parents and sisters have provided unwavering support; Patrice Lawrence played a pivotal role in setting me on the road. Thank you to everyone who spoke to me formally and informally for this book, including my grandad, O.K. Cowan.

Thank you to the Society of Authors for granting me the John C. Lawrence award which enabled me to take two unpaid months off work to finish this book.

Thank you to Micha Frazer for your voice notes and dedicated unionising, a true comrade. Thank you Tamara-Jade and Marissa for your wise inputs – you're still the smartest people I know. Thank you to the team at Anamot Press for your somewhat relentless encouragement.

I am inspired and informed by the writers, thinkers and organisers who are working to break down Britain's borders in different ways: UKBLM, JCWI, SOAS Detainee Support Group (SDS), Marai Larasi, Dorett Jones, Neha Kagal, Huda Jawad, Luke de Noronha, Empty Cages Collective, Community Action on Prison Expansion (CAPE), Docs not Cops, Corporate Watch, Anti-raids Network, Sisters Uncut, United Families & Friends Campaign (UFFC), the London Campaign Against Police and State Violence (LCAPSV), North East London Migrant Action (NELMA), and the New Economy Organisers Network (NEON).

To Daisy, Delia and Soraya: I am eternally grateful for your love and care.

Introduction
Why break down
borders?

'Another world is possible beyond the plunder, exploitation
and expropriation that are the bedrock of liberal democracies.'
– Akwugo Emejulu and Francesca Sobande

'To struggle for a world without borders is to have hope . . . is
to think that human beings can do better, and we do deserve
better.' – Bridget Anderson

Borders are indisputably sites of violence. Borders create citizens
and non-citizens, 'aliens' and nationals, undocumented people
and *sans papiers*, 'foreigners' and expats. Borders segregate, categorise and dehumanise us. They are the product of long histories
of injustice, which means that we – our, flesh, bones and the
very breath which keeps us alive – can be crudely termed 'illegal'
in the eyes of the law. The phrase, 'illegal immigrant', which in
Britain creeps from newspaper headlines to state policies and
back again, encourages us to believe that we can be a violation of
law and order as it is sold to us.

However, laws and order are not objective truths, and borders
have not always existed. Immigration laws, for example, are ideas
crafted in the imaginations of the powerful to maintain their
position and preserve the world as they like it. Borders are not
real. The criminal 'justice' system and its agents such as border

force, prisons and the police – an institution founded to protect private property and break up workers' strikes[1] – all function to uphold laws and protect the status quo of inequality. They do not keep the peace. These structures bring the violence. Laws try to rationalise the border regime which fundamentally ignores the humanity of those who move. Knowing this, let's take as our root and starting position the reality that no human is illegal.

In this book, I draw connecting lines between Britain's murky past and the precarious present of the UK border regime. Through interrogating Britain's imperial history, we can better understand the current context of immigration laws, political agendas and structures of inequality which prop up the border. These chapters explore the purpose and consequences of borders; sometimes imagined as benign geographical markers drawing out where one country ends, and another begins. Through knowing the history, character, and ever-shifting purpose of borders and the agents that enforce them, we can better resist the border and equip ourselves against its impact on us all.

Resistance to the border is complicated. It often involves rejecting borders while at the same time trying to improve the immediate realities of people crossing them, by seeking to reform or soften the border regime. There is here, in this resistance, what author and academic Natasha King calls a 'fundamental tension': sometimes we find ourselves acting within and to an extent validating a system that is harming ourselves and others. This happens when we defend and advocate for people's right to reside or have citizenship, alongside also rejecting the exalted category of 'citizen'.[2] This tension cannot be easily reconciled, which feels apt for the pursuit of human movement

---

1   S. Harring, *Policing A Class Society* (Chicago: Haymarket Books, 2017).

2   N. King, *No Borders: The Politics Of Immigration Control And Resistance* (London: Zed Books, 2016).

and mobility, which is complex and messy. Free movement is so basic, and so intrinsic that it could be described as an inevitable part of the human condition. Underneath it all, movement and border-crossing is so expected as to be banal, but nonetheless our stories of moving and journeying are rich and wondrous in their immense variety and multiple dimensions.

Much like the narratives of many migrant communities, my family's history of border-crossing is archived primarily in the memories of elders, occasionally spoken as oral histories which drop like rare jewels from wise mouths at the dinner table. My paternal grandparents came from Jamaica to the UK in the 1950s as citizens of Britain. They are part of what is termed the 'Windrush generation', named after the *HMT Empire Windrush*, an ex-Nazi ship acquired as a prize of war by Britain, which was charted from the Caribbean to England in 1948. Many more ships followed the *Empire Windrush*. This generation of border-crossers were invited, so the story goes, to help rebuild Britain after the destruction of World War II.

This movement to Britain retraced a trail paved with blood, capital and labour; this homecoming to the mother country was inextricably linked to Jamaica's position as a colony of the British Empire. During the seventeenth and eighteenth centuries, Britain played a leading role in trafficking and enslaving African people, bringing them to countries like Jamaica to labour on plantations and grow and harvest crops like tobacco and later sugar cane. The profits which were extracted from slave labour were invested back in Britain – through the construction of banks, factories and canals which helped industrialisation to flourish.[3] Meanwhile back in Jamaica, in the decades and cen-

---

3   David Eltis and Stanley L. Engerman, 'The Importance of Slavery and the Slave Trade to Industrializing Britain,' *Journal of Economic History*, vol. 60, no. 1, 2000, pp. 123–44, www.jstor.org/stable/2566799.

turies following the abolition of legal slavery, 'freed' Jamaicans subsisted in conditions of poverty, and the country faced slow economic growth and high levels of unemployment and state debt.

Fast forward a hundred or so years to 1952, and my grandfather purchases a one-way ticket to England, hoping to study and secure a better future for his family. He waves goodbye to relatives and loved ones in Jamaica – including my grandmother – promising to send for her if he manages to find a job. When he does find work drilling holes into hob elements, my grandmother takes the long boat journey to join him, with the talisman of a nutmeg nestled in her pocket to remind her of home and to ward off sea-sickness. When she arrives in England in the middle of a frosty winter, she notices the leafless trees, and wonders why all the trees are dead.

This migration route, so steeped in history, was taken by almost half a million Caribbean people between 1948–70, curious to see what Britain was like, and seeking to build lives for themselves and their families. However, the hostile border between Britain and the Caribbean was firmly reasserted in the 1971 Immigration Act, and the expansion of this border continues to the present day. In 2018 the 'Windrush scandal' exposed that British Caribbean elders had been subjected to targeted immigration enforcement by the UK Home Office, as part of government attempts to meet net immigration goals. This is only one example: similar relationships of exploitation, where migrant communities are dismissed once they have served their economic purpose, exist between the UK and countries all over the world.

The history of physical border demarcation is elite, colonial and rooted in capitalism. Borders have always been closely linked to securing property and territory and shoring up wealth.

From the Great Wall of China to Hadrian's Wall in the North of England, early borders around regions and cities were built to preserve empires and keep out 'invaders'. More recent constructions such as the US-Mexico border wall, the apartheid wall in occupied Palestine, and the mile-long wall in Calais in northern France which fortifies the entrance to the Channel Tunnel demonstrate how borders are erected in attempts to preserve ideologies, prevent free movement, and oppress populations.

Around 70 physical border walls now exist globally.[4] This figure rapidly increased after the end of World War II, a point at which only seven border walls had been constructed. The building of border walls also intensified after 9/11, including at the US-Mexico border which was fortified by measures pushed through by George W. Bush's administration, and then developed further under Barack Obama's presidency. The US-Mexico wall continues to be leveraged by politicians of all stripes to symbolise protection of American citizens from 'dangerous' outsiders. Immigration enforcement was ramped up alongside this renewed wall-building fervour: Obama's administration deported more people than the collective sum of deportations carried out by all other US presidents in the twentieth century.[5]

As I illustrate in Chapter 4, politicians and lawmakers' dedication to borders and immigration controls is guided and intensified by the sentiments churned out by national and international media outlets. The strong symbolism of borders is prime fodder for the screaming headlines of the 24-hour news cycle; looming stone and steel fortifications provoke quasi-biblical and mythological connotations. States encourage and respond

---

4   www.nytimes.com/2019/01/17/world/europe/fact-check-trump-border-walls. html (last accessed 08/2020).

5   www.abcnews.go.com/Politics/obamas-deportation-policy-numbers/ story?id=41715661 (last accessed 08/2020).

to this sentiment with enthusiasm. Throughout this book I outline some of the laws and policies that have built up Britain's current border regime: cumulatively they demonstrate that the state will never meaningfully legislate for open, relaxed or no borders, because to do so would be to blur the edges of its own power. Work to amend immigration laws and policies is important insofar as it improves people's lives in the here and now – but we must carefully consider the ways in which 'reforming' an inherently abusive border regime makes it harder to destroy altogether. Just as air inside a balloon would never advocate for bursting the skin that holds it, states as we know them will never support steps towards their own eradication.

Because of the inherent inequality borders represent, in the twenty-first century wealthy white people who move countries and cross borders call themselves 'expats', while working class people including people of colour in particular who make the same journey are framed as 'immigrants'. Borders enable states to manage the flow of people, and consequently surveil, dissuade and shut out people who are perceived by states as less permanently desirable or useful for wealth accumulation: neurodiverse people, queer and trans people, disabled people, survivors of violence, torture and abuse, people with different antibody statuses, people of colour, criminalised people and working class people.

Some of us experience this inequality viscerally when we attempt to cross borders: through harassment and physical searches at ports of entry, to intrusive questioning, extortionate fees and kafkaesque hoops which must be jumped through to obtain visas to visit or work in another country. While white cisgender women influencers gaily post Instagram stories of their passports, artfully propped against a chilled glass of prosecco in the British Airways Business Class lounge, queer and trans

people of colour are interrogated about their 'origin' and identities. Similarly, people profiled and racialised as Arab or Muslim
are scrutinised and accused of terrorism, and people from
formerly colonised countries are handcuffed in the back of a
van, awaiting deportation to a country they have never lived in.
If you have never felt the surveilling eye and iron fist of borders,
it does not mean borders are not violent weapons; it means that
your privilege enables you to circumnavigate the gleaming edge
of their blade.

In Chapters 6 and 7, I further explore the sinister structures of Britain's draconian immigration detention estate and
deportation regime. These aspects of the UK's immigration
enforcement apparatus abuse and violate the human rights
of people of colour, working class people, and people seeking
asylum: members of our communities who are least resourced
to secure legal representation and defend themselves against the
state. Furthermore, this segment of the immigration system is
incredibly costly: in 2013–17 the government spent over £500m
on detaining people,[6] and in 2015 paid £5,000 for each deportation it carried out.[7] This matters, not because we should rely
on the dehumanising 'business case' for ending detention and
deportation, but because these figures throw light on one of the
foundational pillars of detention and deportation: the trade of
human lives for private profit.

While the architects of border controls – states, transna-
tional structures, and private companies largely governed by
middle-aged white men in boardrooms – shore up wealth at the
expense of migrant communities, immigration processes which

6   www.independent.co.uk/news/uk/home-news/uk-immigration-detention-
centre-cost-taxpayer-brexit-eu-migrants-a8195251.html (last accessed 08/2020).

7   www.theyworkforyou.com/wrans/?id=2015-07-14.6908.h&s=charter+flight
#g6908.r0 (last accessed 08/2020).

7

divide and segregate constitute a silencing for the people they impact. Frequently, the threat of incarceration or deportation means that people residing in a state on the basis of a visa with precarious immigration status, or who are undocumented, are dissuaded from speaking out against the actions of that state. The 'good immigrant' narrative relies on migrant communities toeing the line, self-policing and making sure to 'contribute' to the economy while being compliant in state processes.

Certain community groups are given the moniker of 'model minority', as explained by writer Wei Ming Kam,[8] who writes in *The Good Immigrant* that, 'The Chinese in the UK have been called the 'hidden' or 'invisible' community, given that we are perceived as ostensibly successful, assimilated into British society and self-reliant.' This inaccurate homogenising (a 2017 report by the Joseph Rowntree Foundation found that in the past 20 years, consistently 15–20 per cent more Chinese adults in the UK are in poverty than white adults)[9] has a range of impacts. Wei Ming Kam notes that the idea of Chinese people as model minorities stereotypes other migrant communities as loud and not hard-working. It also means that the needs of Chinese communities in Britain, such as access to certain public services and participation in civic life, are not supported.

This is an anxiety-inducing state to exist in, and the sense of security derived from keeping your head down is in many cases tragically revealed to be false. As I detail in Chapter 2, schemes such as Operation Nexus, which target EEA (European Economic Area)[10] citizens in the UK for deportation, demon-

---

8   N. Shukla, *The Good Immigrant* (London: Unbound, 2016).

9   www.jrf.org.uk/sites/default/files/jrf/files-research/uk_poverty_2017.pdf (last accessed September 2020).

10   The European Economic Area (EEA) includes the EU and three members of the European Free Trade Association (EFTA): Iceland, Norway and Liechtenstein.

strate how the shifting goalposts of citizenship mean that the act of sleeping rough, for example, can be used without warning as grounds for being forcibly removed from the country.

At the same time as hindering livelihoods and preventing our free movement, borders and immigration controls also attempt to stem the flow of ideas, stories and histories. Because of this, as communities with migration histories, we must document our experiences and attempt to reclaim our narratives. Having examined how borders were constructed, the violence they enact, and the communities and people they impact throughout this book, in Chapter 7 I ask: how can we resist them? This book exists, in part, in response to institutional attempts to silence migrant communities, to whitewash our presence and erase us from history books. Our shared stories of border resistance can never be laboured enough; while being sites of violence and harm, border-crossing also illuminates our ability to sustain, survive and re-imagine.

When it was exposed in 2018 that the destruction of Windrush landing cards which date-stamped the arrival of Caribbean elders to Britain had been signed off under the Labour government, and operationalised by Theresa May as Home Secretary, the vital importance of documenting our own histories was re-emphasised. We have never and can never rely on the British state to archive our narratives: throughout my work on this topic I have drawn on the careful record-making and research of the Black Cultural Archives, the Migration Museum, the International Slavery Museum, the Institute of Race Relations, Black History Walks, refugeehistory.org, and the Legacy of British Slave-Ownership research project at UCL, among others. By capturing and commemorating our migration histories we become the architects of what is known about us, and how we are remembered by our communities and those committed to the dismantling of borders.

Being a British passport-holder and documented person affords me the privilege to move through academic institutions and numerous workplaces, which has enabled me to study and write about border-crossing. Because of this, it is of vital importance that my work is guided by and rooted in the knowledge and expertise of people experiencing the sharp end of border violence – including comrades and freedom fighters I have worked in solidarity with in UK detention centres. I would encourage you to look to places like Detained Voices, which publishes verbatim testimony given by people in UK detention centres, and the Step Up Migrant Women campaign which fights for access to support for migrant survivors of violence in the UK. This book is effective only as an accompaniment to the voices and writings of those leading the struggle against borders globally. I write this in recognition of and respect for the labour and organising of migrant communities past and present, and for my ancestors who were brought in chains to Jamaica, and despite the oppressive shadow of the British Empire nurtured the seedlings of our family tree. I write now, as I always have, so our stories and bloodshed do not run into the dust. Because our survival knows no boundary, our resistance will be a tale everlasting.

Chapter 1

In the shadow of the British Empire

'Britain made 1/3 of the world one big Ol' Empire, enslaved our ancestors and now here we are. Is that what [we] should be "grateful" for?' – Kimberly McIntosh

Britain often thinks of itself as a small island: a modest vessel bobbing bravely in uncharted seas, a sturdy albeit unseasoned sandwich at the smorgasbord of many. However, this 'small island' claim is a clever deception. It is a distraction – a sly smile hiding rows of razor-sharp teeth, stained with the blood-soaked details of a murky history. Nonetheless, Britain's 'small island' defence has been invoked throughout history to defend ever more exclusionary attitudes towards newcomers.

Out of around 195 countries which make up the world, the United Kingdom is the 79th largest, around half the size of Spain and a third of the size of Nigeria. Despite its modest ranking, Britain is the ninth richest country in the world. Economically speaking, considering its size, the UK is punching above its category. The country is both rich and resilient: armed to the teeth with an annual defence budget of £41bn, as well as using other pots of money to further galvanise its borders, such as the

£4bn[1] allocated to pull up the drawbridge and prepare to leave the European Union (EU) during Brexit (Britain's departure from the EU).

The inconvenient reality is that gentle Britannia has, at one point or another, invaded 90 per cent of the world.[2] Britain's exploits – violently and illicitly extracting resources and labour from other countries while seeking to decimate social, spiritual and cultural systems in order to galvanise its place in the world order – have made it an incredibly wealthy nation.

The term imperialism describes the way in which one country seeks to extend its power or control in the world. Imperialism comes in different shapes and sizes. For example, Britain's imperial activities have included or currently include 'colonising' or taking control of a country and the people living in it; invading a country or region using military force, and in various other ways indirectly controlling the political or economic activities of a country.

Who gets to 'explore' and 'discover' new lands?

Despite the inherent violence it entails, imperialism and colonialism are often conceptualised and repackaged using much softer terminology, such as exploration and discovery. In part this is due to the fields of history, economics, sociology and more being largely dominated by the perspectives and writings of colonisers themselves, and white men in general. This isn't just a historical imbalance which can be attributed to women's

---

1 https://assets.publishing.service.gov.uk/government/uploads/system/uploads/attachment_data/file/752202/Budget_2018_red_web.pdf#page=31 (last accessed 08/2020).

2 www.theatlantic.com/international/archive/2012/11/british-have-invaded-90-percent-countries-earth/321789/ (last accessed 08/2020).

absence from formal research and publishing in previous centuries: as recently as 2015, the US online journal *Slate* reported that in a sample of 614 popular history titles, 75.8 per cent were written by men. The UK doesn't fare much better: in the top 50 best-selling history titles in the same year, only four were written by women, all of whom are white.[3] The impact of this is that the way we understand historical events and their legacies are, for the most part, framed around narrow perspectives which are imbued with privilege and wealth.

For example, the British 'explorer' Captain James Cook who claims to have 'discovered' Australia in the eighteenth century is described on the website of the Greenwich Royal Museums as 'controversial' but also a 'national hero'.[4] The controversy mentioned refers to Cook's violent oppression of the indigenous communities he encountered. Armed conflict and discriminatory policies spearheaded by Cook led to the decimation of thousands of indigenous Australians, as well as the spread of European diseases such as smallpox, measles, typhus, and cholera which ravaged communities with no previous exposure or immunity to them. Poor record-keeping and a general lack of respect for indigenous lives by settlers means that it is difficult to get a sense of how many people died in this period. Massacres that were recorded describe indigenous Australians, including children, being shot, beheaded, pushed off cliffs and dragged through fire, for 'crimes' that read very plainly as attempts to survive such as taking back corn, clothing, cattle and sheep.

---

3   www.theguardian.com/books/2016/jan/11/popular-history-writing-remains-a-male-preserve-publishing-study-finds (last accessed 08/2020).

4   www.rmg.co.uk/discover/explore/exploration-endeavour/captain-james-cook (last accessed 08/2020).

Writing about Cook's arrival in Australia for the British Library's online article collection, Aboriginal language and culture consultant Dr Shayne T. Williams reflects:

[Cook's arrival] is symbolic because it portended the end of our cultural dominion over our lands. Not surprisingly, discussion of Cook's landing sparks a sadness among my peoples – a sadness that laments Cook's voyage, precipitating some 18 years later, the landing of the First Fleet (1788). With the First Fleet came the legal fiction terra nullius, a fiction that was applied to justify colonial subjugation of us.[5]

The term *terra nullius* means 'no one's land', which is how Cook described Australia on his arrival: void of inhabitants or owners. This is often how colonialism is framed – the 'civilising' of lands that aren't meeting their 'potential'. *Terra nullius* provided the supposed legal basis for Cook to seize the land and declare it British property. In reality, Australia was already inhabited when Cook arrived, but his arrival marked a devastating new era: by the 1920s, 90 per cent of the indigenous population in Australia had been killed.[6] The claim of *terra nullius* is another example of British colonial interference being framed as a noble mission – to populate and nurture the 'wasteland' of Australia – but of course the reality of imperialism is not all rustic scenes of tilling the land. Aboriginal lawman Hobbles Danayarri describes Cook's arrival as marking the beginning of the slaughter of indigenous people, dispossession of land, and forced low-paid labour or servitude. In spite of this, Danayarri generously and strategically

5   www.bl.uk/the-voyages-of-captain-james-cook/articles/an-indigenous-australian-perspective-on-cooks-arrival (last accessed 08/2020).
6   www.nationalarchives.gov.uk/education/empire/g2/cs2/background.htm (last accessed 08/2020).

advocated for hospitality to be shown to the violent invaders, remarking 'This a big country, and we been mix em up [people]. We're on this land now. We can be friendly, join in, be friends, mates, together.'[7]

Much of British colonialism and expansionism is framed and justified as a plucky voyage into lands that are either under-utilised by indigenous people, or simply empty, unclaimed and ripe for the taking. This rhetoric isn't just dusty words from old parchment written by people in a different time. Boris Johnson, the UK's prime minister at the time of writing, wrote in *The Sun* in 2002 that 'The best fate for Africa would be if the old colonial powers [. . .] scrambled once again in her direction.' In the *Spectator* he wrote of the continent, 'The problem is not that we were once in charge, but that we are not in charge any more.' Johnson is not alone among Britain's political elite in his nostalgia for the days when the sun never set on the Empire. Much campaigning and commentary around Brexit has played on concepts of sovereignty. This idea is based on an appetite for Britain to go it alone, like in the 'good old days', and according to civil servants working on Brexit, hopes to bring about 'Empire 2.0' by rebuilding trading partnerships with the Commonwealth.[8]

This golden-era thinking conveniently overlooks a crucial detail: that slavery was abolished and colonialism in its primary form overthrown by the rebellion of people living in the colonies, in dialogue with British dissidents who were resisting in the hub of the Empire. Because of this, there shall be no easy return. Priyamvada Gopal, whose book *Insurgent Empire* maps out the role of uprisings in booting out colonial rule, remarks that: 'It's

---

7   http://adb.anu.edu.au/biography/danayarri-hobbles-12397 (last accessed 08/ 2020).

8   The Commonwealth is a coalition of formerly colonised countries, which was set up in 1931.

very important to recover the history of violence that colonialism entailed, but also the history of opposition to that violence in Britain.' Where former colonial subjects or enslaved people freed themselves from their own shackles, states rained down punishment and further control. For example, in 1825 the modern-day equivalent of $21bn was extorted from Haiti by France, as 'repayment' for the successful 1804 slave rebellion against French colonial rule. Trinidadian writer and socialist C. L. R. James chronicles in *The Black Jacobins* that this rebellion blew up in the wake of the French Revolution and the storming of the Bastille, setting the stage for liberation movements from Africa to the Caribbean. The potency of these movements are often pushed to the footnotes of history, but should never be underestimated.

Colonialism and imperialism are important parts of migration histories, because the flow of capital within and across borders is intrinsically tied to the movement of people. The hidden history of Britain's resource-grabbing global gadabouts is both buried deep in the British psyche, and somehow all around us. From the roads we drive along, which historically were coated with asphalt stolen from Trinidad, to the proliferation of sugar through slave labour which sweetens a cup of English breakfast tea, the legacy of colonialism cannot be escaped.[9]

The 'white man's burden'

Imperialism can sometimes be insidious and hard to detect from the outside. In Akala's 2018 book *Natives: Race and Class in the Ruins of Empire*, he writes that 'No one refers to the "white man's burden" any more, as it's just too crude a phrase, so instead we

---

9   More information about this can be found via Black History Walks (www.blackhistorywalks.co.uk).

speak of spreading democracy and human rights and of saving people from dictators.' The phrase 'white man's burden' takes its name from a poem by British journalist and author Rudyard Kipling, who wrote with his whole chest that the white man's burden is 'the business of introducing a sane and orderly administration to the dark places of the earth'. The phrase is now used as a wry short-hand to refer to European colonists' oppressive viewpoint that imperialism was a noble civilising mission. The 2003 invasion of Iraq by Britain and the US is just one pertinent example of this new or 'neo-' imperialism in action.

The invasion of Iraq was framed by then US president George W. Bush in a radio address as a benevolent mission to 'disarm Iraq of weapons of mass destruction, to end Saddam Hussein's support for terrorism, and to free the Iraqi people'.[10] It later transpired that the US did not actually have intelligence on any alleged weapons of mass destruction.[11] Furthermore, alongside allegedly 'freeing' people in Iraq, British and US forces killed an estimated 2.4 million Iraqi people,[12] including a reported 200,000 civilians.[13] In a 2003 House of Commons debate, then UK prime minister Tony Blair roundly dismissed as a 'conspiracy theory', suggestions that the proposed invasion of Iraq was in fact not motivated by the pursuit of freedom and liberty, but driven by a desire to seize control of Iraq's plentiful oil fields. Blair countered with the not entirely reassuring statement that 'if oil were the issue, [it would] be infinitely simpler to cut a deal with Saddam, who, I am sure, would be delighted to give

10   https://georgewbush-whitehouse.archives.gov/news/releases/2003/03/20030322.html (last accessed 08/2020).

11   www.vox.com/2016/7/9/12123022/george-w-bush-lies-iraq-war (last accessed 08/2020).

12   www.stopwar.org.uk/index.php/news-comment/2931-the-iraq-death-toll-15-years-after-the-us-invasion (last accessed 08/2020).

13   www.iraqbodycount.org/ (last accessed 08/2020).

us access to as much oil as we wanted'. It became clear that the freedom-fighting invasion of Iraq was in fact driven by imperial motivations: desires to extend US and British power over the region.

The tentacles of Britain's colonial dealings are far-reaching, and its impacts continue to reverberate around the globe in the present day. In the first half of 2019 alone, unrest boiled over in Sudan, Kashmir and Hong Kong; all of which have colonial connections to Britain. Conflicts between North and South Sudan have existed since the end of the nineteenth century, when Britain implemented a 'divide and rule' policy to prevent people in Sudan from forming a united front against colonial rulers.[14] When South Sudan gained independence in 2011 a period of unrest began, and in December 2018 protests broke out drawing attention to unlivable economic conditions amplified by the partition of Sudan. In June 2019, a sit-in in the capital city of Khartoum ended in mass violence when Rapid Support forces surrounded the protest and beat and tortured hundreds of protestors. Reflecting on the sit-in, Dena Latif writes for *gal-dem*:

> The sit-in was beautiful, not only because it represented freedom, but because it embraced and unified people of every ethnicity, religion, class and gender. Every government Sudan has ever known, starting with the colonial Anglo-Egyptian Condominium, has worked to divide-and-rule us. Our differences, from skin colour to language, have been exacerbated and manipulated by regimes to reinforce their own power as they installed tribal hierarchies.[15]

14   www.sudantribune.com/Roots-of-Sudanese-conflict-are-in,25558 (last accessed 08/2020).

15   http://gal-dem.com/the-revolutionary-sudan-sit-in-has-been-destroyed-but-weve-come-too-far-to-turn-back/ (last accessed 08/2020).

A 2019 parliamentary briefing on asylum statistics showed that in 2015, people from Sudan formed the second largest nationality granted asylum in the UK, with 'armed conflict between the Government and rebels' one of the key reasons given for seeking sanctuary.[16] Britain has colonised, controlled or influenced all but five countries in the world;[17] it is evident that Britain's interference on the global stage has lit the touch paper for so many of the conflicts that have emerged since.

Current neo-imperial projects are more likely to take the form of government spending being framed as 'humanitarian aid' to achieve political and economic objectives in other countries. In 2016 it was revealed that Priti Patel, then International Development Secretary, and at the time of writing the UK's Home Secretary, planned to use £11bn of foreign aid to bolster trade deals in advance of Britain's exit from the EU.[18] Similarly, in 2012 the G7 (an international economic organisation comprised of seven wealthy countries: Canada, France, Germany, Italy, Japan, the UK and the US) created the New Alliance for Food Security and Nutrition, a body tasked with helping along corporate investment in African countries. According to trade and anti-poverty charity Global Justice Now, in return for aid from the New Alliance, African countries have had to 'make changes in their land, seed and trade rules, handing control over to big business at the expense of small-scale farmers'.[19] The impact of the New Alliance's 'aid' money is that small-scale farmers lose access to water, seeds and land as massive profit-hungry multi-

---

16   https://old.parliament.uk/briefing-papers/sn01403.pdf (last accessed 08/2020).

17   www.vox.com/2014/6/24/5835320/map-in-the-whole-world-only-these-five-countries-escaped-european (last accessed 08/2020).

18   www.telegraph.co.uk/news/2016/07/30/britain-to-leverage-11bn-of-foreign-aid-to-build-new-trade-deals/ (last accessed 08/2020).

19   www.globaljustice.org.uk/sites/default/files/files/resources/growing_evidence_against_the_new_alliance_.pdf (last accessed 08/2020).

national companies such as Monsanto and Unilever wade in and take control of food production. Colonial projects, then, have simply shape-shifted. Rather than using its wealth to address the deep-rooted global inequality it has played a key role in creating, British governments consistently use money as a bargaining chip to exert power and influence.

The context of Britain's imperial past matters, because the colonial projects and the wealth Britain extracted from them set the stage for the settlement of migrant communities in the UK. Colonisation creates bonds that tie in both directions. More broadly, the process of colonialism boosted economic growth in the Global North, and in many cases depressed wealth in the Global South.[20] This has created a scenario where the very communities who have experienced oppression as Britain shores up wealth through the pillaging of their labour and resources, are asked to prove, again, their worth and to 'contribute' when they arrive on Britain's shores.

---

20   The terms 'Global North' and 'Global South' are used to differentiate between countries with a high economic output (due to being the architects of colonialism and neo-imperialism), the majority of which are situated in the northern hemisphere (hence Global 'North'), and those with a lower economic output, the majority of which are situated in tropical regions and the southern hemisphere (hence Global 'South'). This terminology is acknowledged to be simplistic, however, it provides a less hierarchical and derogatory alternative to the problematic dichotomies of 'developing country/developed country' and 'third world/first world'.

Chapter 2

Whitewashing and the myth of the migrant 'outsider'

'We managed. Somehow or other, you do. You didn't have any choice, did you?' – elder from the Windrush generation, reflecting on life in 1950s Britain

Living in a country that is seemingly, constantly itching to find a way back to some mythical, long-lost white monocultural yesteryear is exhausting. Still, we persist in the face of intense violence and marginalisation, a word I use to describe the process by which people are pushed to the edges of existence so that they cannot live free and full lives. I think of my grandfather, who walked the streets at night after a long factory shift, going door-to-door to find someone who would rent a room to him and my grandmother. He came to the 'mother country' a citizen, and in the face of twitching curtains and locked doors, found a way through. The slogan used by the Zapatistas in the 1990s,[1] and more recently by Mexican activists in the face of corrupt police

---

1   The Zapatistas are a Mexican revolutionary indigenous-led movement. They formed in 1983 and continue to fight for protections and justice for the indigenous peoples of Mexico.

assassinations (borrowing from Greek poet Dinos Christianop-
oulos) rings true for all people struggling in hostile lands: 'They
tried to bury us. They didn't know we were seeds.'

The way that public discussions around migration are navi-
gated could give the impression that the movement of people
to the UK is a brand new concept; an alarming upward trend
in need of nipping in the bud. This couldn't be further from
the truth. While the majority of migration to the UK has
happened since the Second World War ended in 1945,[2] migrant
communities and people of colour have existed in the UK for
many centuries. In *Staying Power*, Peter Fryer's comprehensive
chronicle of black British history published in 1984, he notes
that 'Africans and Asians and their descendants – have been
living in Britain for close on 500 years.'[3] Fryer also notes that
there were African people living in Britain even before English
people arrived, as soldiers in the Roman army. These histories
and many more, compiled by British writers and historians
such as Fryer and his contemporaries David Olusoga, Emma
Dabiri, Priyamvada Gopal, Reni Eddo-Lodge and more, challenge contemporary perspectives on migration to Britain. They
evidence that migrant communities and people of colour are
intrinsic to 'Britishness', and their research confirms migration
to the British Isles to be a tale as old as time. The intensity of
anti-migrant sentiment which escalated in the latter half of the
twentieth century and charged with feverish velocity into the
twenty-first century can be seen then as a comparatively new
and utterly jarring invention.

---

2   Although, it's worth noting that between 1964 (when the Office for National
Statistics started collecting comprehensive migration data) and 1983, more people
emigrated from (left) Britain than arrived in Britain from another country.

3   P. Fryer, *Staying Power: The History of Black People in Britain* (London: Pluto Press,
2010).

The entire history of migration to Britain is of course far too sizable to comprehensively detail in this book. Nonetheless, we can explore a few periods within our rich history to help sketch out the development of Britain as a border nation – a place defined as much by who is kept out as who and what is allowed in. To be clear: these examples should not be interpreted as suggesting that people do not have agency in their own journeys, and that every migration is in some way dictated by Britain. Rather, they seek to show that positioning migrants as 'outsiders', or of having no real connection to Britain is entirely ahistorical. Understanding this reality exposes the absurdity of requiring migrants to 'contribute' to Britain and its economy in order to justify our residence here. These examples show how, in fact, Britain owes so much to so many communities and countries, who have, largely through force and coercion, expended labour, spilt blood, and lost lives in Britain's pursuit of wealth and power.

One migration story which has gained renewed popular interest in the past few years is that of the 'Windrush generation' of Caribbean people who came to the UK in the latter part of the twentieth century. In June 1948, the *HMT Empire Windrush* docked at Tilbury in Essex, marking the first significant wave of immigration from the Caribbean, in particular Jamaica, Trinidad and Tobago, Barbados, and St Lucia. The Windrush generation arrived in Britain between 1948 and the early 1970s not as immigrants but as citizens, due to the 1948 British Nationality Act which granted full citizenship to people living in British colonies (countries that would later comprise the Commonwealth).

The context of this migration route is centuries older. For example, in 1655 England colonised Jamaica during a naval invasion launched by Oliver Cromwell and held power in the country until independence in 1962. During the seventeenth and eighteenth centuries, Britain transported enslaved people from West Africa to Jamaica – a 'forced migration' – to labour on plantations growing cotton and tobacco. These industries were later replaced with the growing and harvesting of sugarcane, which led British-ruled Jamaica to become the most prolific exporter of sugar in all of the colonies.

The violence of colonial curriculums

The heavy-handed British propaganda machine cranked up a few gears in the Caribbean colonies from the moment of formal 'emancipation' from slavery in the late 1830s, which marked the ending of legal ownership of another person (but not the end of enslavement in practice). During this period, reformers and abolitionists decided that educating formerly enslaved people – largely with glorified myths about Britain – was the best way to keep society stable. Dr Ruby King, a historian based at the University of the West Indies, notes that prominent abolition-ist the second Earl Grey raised concerns about how to convince formerly enslaved people to keep labouring on plantations once they were freed.[4] In a memorandum he wrote that: 'the great problem to be solved in drawing up any plan for the emancipa-tion of the slaves [was] to devise some mode of inducing them [. . .] to undergo the regular and continuous labor which [was] indispensable in carrying on the production of sugar'.[5] Subse-quently, a 'morally rigorous', Christian education system was gradually implemented as a form of social control.

An Anglo-centric curriculum reinforced the idea that Brit-ain's colonies and its 'subjects' should always see themselves as

---

4   www.educoas.org/Portal/bdigital/contenido/interamer/BkIACD/Interamer/Interamerhtml/Millerhtml/mil_mil.htm#* (last accessed 08/2020).

5   E. Williams, *Columbus to Castro: The History of the Caribbean 1492–1969* (London: André Deutsch, 1970).

thus – people existing in relation to, and dependent on Britain. The white-washing of history, geography, and literature lessons in the Caribbean (as in Britain) sought to teach students that their countries began with and were made significant by British governance. The impact of these lessons intended to have a damp-ening effect on Caribbean peoples' capacity to rebuild a sense of distinct personal and national identity in the wake of slavery.

Similarly, British politicians in India during the period of colonisation (between the early 1600s and 1947) campaigned hard to suppress and eradicate Indian languages and teachings. Thomas Macaulay, the British Secretary at War and a member of the supreme council of the East India Company,[6] played a key role in the violent imposition of the English language and British curricula in India in the 1830s. Macaulay's oppres-sive approach to 'education' led to the coining of the concept of 'Macaulayism' – the systematic destruction of indigenous cultural thought and practices through the implementation of new education systems. In a document sent by Macaulay to the supreme council in 1835, known as the Macaulay 'Minute on Indian education' he wrote:

the dialects commonly spoken among the natives of this part of India contain neither literary nor scientific informa-tion, and are moreover so poor and rude that, until they are enriched from some other quarter, it will not be easy to trans-late any valuable work into them. [7]

---

6   According to Encyclopedia Britannica, the East India Company was an 'English company formed for the exploitation of trade with East and Southeast Asia and India [. . .] and acted as an agent of British imperialism in India from the early eighteenth century to the mid-nineteenth century'.

7   www.columbia.edu/itc/mealac/pritchett/00generallinks/macaulay/txt_minute_education_1835.html (last accessed 08/2020).

In the same text he asserted that 'a single shelf of a good European library was worth the whole native literature of India and Arabia'. A month after its publication, the Macaulay minute was signed as a resolution, which meant that it would steer future education policy.

The Macaulay minute is a key example of the role that colonial education systems play in British imperial oppression and the justification of its border. As post-colonial revolutionary and critical theorist, Frantz Fanon explained in his 1952 book *Black Skin, White Masks*, European languages are a key tool of colonisation. The introduction of English, which is deeply connected to the creation of whiteness, by force forged a relationship between Britain and the countries it colonised. Similarly, Fanon writes that '[A black person from] Antilles[8] will be proportionately whiter – that is, he will come closer to being a real human being – in direct ratio to his mastery of the French language [. . .] Mastery of language affords remarkable power'.[9]

The impacts of colonialism on formerly colonised countries varies significantly between locations. Economists acknowledge that the process of colonialism paved the way for varying 'institutional legacies'[10] around the world, which in turn provided differing contexts for economic development. Again, it's crucial to interrogate the way economists examine the 'impact' of colonialism; for example, Acemoğlu and Robinson write that in North America, colonisation created societies with 'far more inclusive institutions than in the colonising country itself' and set the scene for 'immense current prosperity'. This perspec-

---

8   Fanon refers to the French Antilles: Guadeloupe and Martinique which were colonised by France; part of Saint Martin (which is partially a constituent country of the Netherlands) and Saint Barthélemy (in English: St Barts).

9   F. Fanon, *Black Skin, White Masks* (New York: Grove Press, 1967).

10   https://voxeu.org/article/economic-impact-colonialism (last accessed 08/2020).

tive appears to minimise the existence of indigenous economic activity – such as cultivating and trading maize, a crop which generates \$75bn a year for the US economy[11] – and glosses over the fact that this 'immense prosperity' does not extend to indigenous communities, around a quarter of whom live in poverty[12] (compared to 11.8 per cent of the non-indigenous population).[13]

Throughout history, the genocide of indigenous and colonised people is presented as – at worst – unfortunate collateral damage in the project of economic development. Whatever way you slice it, from the 1919 Amritsar massacre, when British Indian troops murdered over 1,000 people during a peaceful protest against the arrest of two national leaders, to the suppression and torture of rebels during the Kenyan Mau Mau uprising against colonial rule in the 1950s, the overarching take-home is that the British Empire and its agents lacerated communities, societies, and economies.

Motherland calling

What UK governments didn't appreciate is how their interference in other countries, and self-aggrandising operations might, in different ways, lead to people living in the colonies wanting to move to the wealthy hub of the Empire: Britain. The popular narrative surrounding the Windrush generation, for example, is that in 1948 Britain opened up its doors and invited people from the Caribbean to come and help rebuild the country in

---

11   https://grains.org/study-corn-exports-add-74-7-billion-to-u-s-economy/ (last accessed 08/2020).

12   www.pewresearch.org/fact-tank/2014/06/13/1-in-4-native-americans-and-alaska-natives-are-living-in-poverty/ (last accessed 08/2020).

13   www.census.gov/library/publications/2019/demo/p60-266.html (last accessed 08/2020).

the wake of the devastation of the Second World War. This 'call from the motherland' came at a time when the working population in Britain had plummeted by 1.38 million between 1945–6.[14] This drop is attributed to married women and new retirees leaving their wartime jobs, and families emigrating to Canada, Australia, New Zealand and South Africa – sometimes referred to as the Old Commonwealth, but perhaps more aptly described as the White Commonwealth. However, the 'open door' narrative is a little murkier than it seems as first glance; despite the passing of the 1948 Nationality Act, the government had concerns about the arrival of Caribbean people on Britain's shores. As David Olusoga writes in the *Guardian* in 2018: 'Even before the *Windrush* had left Jamaica, the prime minister, Clement Attlee, had examined the possibility of preventing its embarkation or diverting the ship and the migrants on board to East Africa.'[15]

As is typical with migration, many of the new arrivals ended up taking low-skilled jobs in order to begin earning money. My grandfather found himself in a similar situation. Despite having ambitions to study medicine, with only five pounds in his pocket – enough for a week's board – he talked his way into a job working on a drilling machine. He once explained the situation to me very simply: 'I had to work, I had to live, so the best thing was to try and work in a factory.' Fryer writes that: 'Almost half the men [who came from the Caribbean] (46 per cent) and over a quarter of the women (27 per cent) were skilled manual workers. Yet the newcomers found themselves in most cases

---

14 www.bl.uk/windrush/articles/how-caribbean-migrants-rebuilt-britain# (last accessed 08/2020).

15 www.theguardian.com/commentisfree/2018/apr/22/windrush-story-not-a-rosy-one-even-before-ship-arrived (last accessed 08/2020).

having to settle for a lower job status than they had enjoyed at home. This indeed was their "first big disappointment".[16]

Many Caribbean women came to Britain in response to a dedicated recruitment drive for nurses to work in the newly established National Health Service (NHS). However, Caribbean women who managed to get a job still faced discrimination and struggled to secure adequate conditions in the workplace, which reflected the contempt migrant communities faced in society at large. This is more than a historical issue: during the early months of the Covid-19 pandemic in the UK in 2020, people of colour working in healthcare reported being forced to work without adequate protective equipment, and the *Guardian* reported that by April 2020, 68% of healthcare workers in Britain who had died of the virus were people of colour.[17]

In spite of their precarious working environments, Caribbean workers joined strikes throughout the Winter of Discontent in the late 1970s, and unionised at higher rates than their white counterparts.[18] In a 1975 edition of *Race Today*,[19] a Caribbean woman hospital worker reflects on her experiences protesting against a decision to close 48 NHS beds in her hospital:

Eight of us met with government representatives, five of us were West Indian women. I went to negotiate and sat and heard what the other side had to say. I had to tell one

---

16 Fryer, *Staying Power*.

17 www.theguardian.com/world/2020/apr/16/data-on-bame-deaths-from-covid-19-must-be-published-politicians-warn (last accessed 08/2020).

18 T. Martin-López, *The Winter Of Discontent: Myth, Memory, and History* (Oxford: Oxford University Press, 2014).

19 *Race Today* was a mouthpiece for radical black organising and was published from 1974–88 by the Race Today Collective, a UK-based campaigning organisation which supported anti-colonial grassroots movements fighting for Black Power and women's liberation.

of them that I was not fighting for money but for my people out there. I asked how he would feel if he fell ill and could not get a bed at the hospital because none was available. He mumbled something and I warned him not to talk to me at the back of his teeth. 'Speak up and say what you have to say', I said to him. I give as much as I get. They were forced to compromise and 14 NHS beds were kept open.

Rural workers from India and Pakistan also came to Britain to work in the early 1950s and were encouraged to make the journey by the British government, which was eager to supplement the dwindling workforce with 'willing hands'. For many, the motivation to migrate was indirectly or directly rooted in violent British interference in their home country. Fryer writes that after the Partition of India in 1947,[20] 'millions had found themselves adrift without homes or jobs [. . .] Emigration to Britain offered the prospect of a new life unthreatened by flood, famine, or the miserable poverty that was their countries' chief legacy from imperial rule'. The abrupt and violent partition of 'British India' into India and Pakistan in August 1947 by British colonisers directly led to the deaths of up to 2 million people, and the displacement of 14 million people.[21] It is commonly acknowledged that British involvement in India and

20   The border of India and Pakistan was defined in 1947 by British lawyer and viscount Cyril John Radcliffe, who had famously never been 'east of Paris'. The drawing of the 'Radcliffe Line' caused intense violence and the largest ever forced migration of people not attributed to a natural disaster. The event of Partition created the countries East Pakistan (which gained independence as Bangladesh in 1971), India and West Pakistan. Partition was followed by the annexation of Jammu and Kashmir, a region in which violence had also broken out along religious lines during Partition and beyond.

21   United Nations High Commissioner for Refugees (UNHCR), *The State Of The World's Refugees: Fifty Years Of Humanitarian Action* (Oxford: Oxford University Press, 2000).

the implementation of colonial policies also worked to exacerbate communal tensions which boiled over when British rule was overturned.

The splitting up of the country by Britain was at the time devised along religious lines: the 1951 Census revealed that during and after Partition, millions of people crossed from Muslim-majority Pakistan to Hindu and Sikh-majority India and vice versa. The waves of violence which accompanied mass displacement of communities were unprecedented. Academic Chandni Saxena notes that, among other spates of unrest, riots dubbed 'The Rape of Rawalpindi' resulted in the mass killing of Hindus and Sikhs, and many women threw themselves into fires and wells after killing their daughters to prevent them from being subjected to sexual violence. Similarly, in Delhi in September 1947, large scale anti-Muslim violence and the murder of Muslim refugees was reported.

As in conflicts globally throughout history, women were particular targets for violence, and Saxena notes that

> These women, during partition of India, became bearers of their religion, its honour and sanctity [. . .] They were subjected to such ethnic violence which not only violated their religious community but also sought to 'cleanse' a particular area from the residuals of the warring community.[22]

Women were subjected to beatings, public gang-rape, branding of their genitals and maiming of breasts as a symbolic removal

---

22   Chandni Saxena, 'Dimensions and dynamics of violence during partition of India,' Proceedings of the Indian History Congress. Vol 74, (2013), pp. 909–20, jstor. org/stable/44158892. Chandni Saxena, 'On religion and its implications on women during partition of India,' Proceedings of the Indian History Congress. Vol 75 Platinum Jubilee, (2014), pp.1253–71, jstor.org/stable/44158517.

of their reproductive capacity. The history of British border and colonial sexual violence against South Asian women is extensive.

Having survived the living nightmare of British-enacted partition and the resultant waves of unrest, in the 1970s when Indian women arrived at Heathrow in London, at least 80 and likely more were subjected to a degrading and invasive vaginal examination dubbed the 'virginity test'. The purpose of the invasive examination was to establish whether they were unmarried based on whether their hymens were 'intact', as only women travelling to the UK to live with a fiance were able to come into the UK without a visa. This procedure was humiliating, misogynistic and biologically unsound. It is evident that Britain's colonial interference in countries around the world has a long-reaching and replicating legacy.

Such was the case in the 1970s, when 27,000 Ugandan Asian people who had been expelled from Uganda by dictator Idi Amin arrived in Britain seeking refuge. Writing for *gal-dem* on Idi Amin's oppressive campaign, Amita Joshi explains:

> Uganda being under British rule between 1894 and 1962 meant many citizens had British passports and had been taught English. Many who were politically astute decided to flee the country as they saw increased violence. It was my grandparents luckiest move to go in May. In August 1972, Idi declared British passport-holding Indians, some 40,000 residents, were to leave the country in 90 days. It was another of his purges.

Before the British arrived, Uganda had been comprised of several kingdoms which had a diversified economy, a well-developed governance structure,[23] and which held a dominant trade position

---

23 Hizaamu Ramadhan, 'Analysis of the pre-colonial, colonial and post colonial bureaucracy of Buganda: The major milestones in its development,' Vol.12, (6), (August 2018), pp. 100–109.

due to its salt mines (controlled by the kingdom of Bunyoro).[24] British colonial rule in Uganda began with the establishment of the Uganda Protectorate in 1894, and the decades which followed were characterised by Britain relentlessly extracting taxes and resources from the country. In the early part of the twentieth century, support for colonial projects came in many different guises; a 1922 House of Lords debate illustrates this well. The Lords met to debate taxation in the colonies of Kenya and Uganda, with the speakers raising concerns that the level of taxation was too high. In the debate, it is clear that the Lords' fear is not that heavy taxation is decimating Ugandan peoples' standard of living, but that as Lord Hindlip states, taxes have 'absolutely crippled the purchasing power of the natives, and [. . .] made impossible the importation of European goods'.[25] In the discussion, Ugandans are perceived primarily as sources of income and profit, and the economic case for colonialism is presented. However, the Archbishop of Canterbury Randall Davidson interjects with an attempt to bring some 'morality' into the discussion, reminding those present that:

> Our sole justification for the place that we hold in Africa, is the benefit of the people, of those men and women to whom the land, the trees and the rest to which we have been referring really belong. It is their affair, and our business is, as a great trust, to help them to make more of the land which is theirs.[26]

The Archbishop's position is one of 'paternalism', a dictatorial position which sees subjugation of people living in the colonies

---

24   www.africa.upenn.edu/NEH/uhistory.htm (last accessed 08/2020).

25   https://api.parliament.uk/historic-hansard/lords/1922/may/10/taxation-in-kenya-colony-and-uganda (last accessed 08/2020).

26   Ibid.

– what he refers to in the same debate as 'the child races, the backward races of the world' – as a kindness. This is the same justification used by Captain James Cook in the eighteenth century, when he describes Australia as an under-used 'no one's land'. The myths and stories which maintain colonialism and inequality, which is the fundamental basis for borders, are deep-rooted. Equally, the continuing exploitation of other countries as a source of profit is barely concealed in the present day.

Who can claim Britishness?

Moving into the second half of the twentieth century, by the time the Conservative government's 1981 British Nationality Act is brought in, the demographic of Britain has changed forever. The 1981 Act is arguably introduced in response to this population change, as sociology professor Imogen Tyler explains: 'it was an Immigration Act designed to define, limit and remove the entitlements to citizenship from British nationals in the Commonwealth (the former colonies) thereby restricting immigration to the British Isles and creating 'aliens' within the borders of the nation state'.[27] The 1981 Act removed the principles of birth-right citizenship, which meant that being born in the UK was no longer 'enough' to claim citizenship.

This shift from 'soil' to 'blood' as the basis upon which citizenship could be claimed was underscored by the right-wing government's racist ideology which saw whiteness and Britishness as being inextricably linked. The Act gave some Commonwealth citizens the right to register as British citizens – at the time a process which incurred a fee, and had no tangible benefit so many didn't engage in it and later struggled to prove

---

27 www.tandfonline.com/doi/full/10.1080/13621020903466357 (last accessed 08/2020).

their residency right. The 1981 Act fitted neatly onto a trajectory which had gathered speed in the preceding decades: in 1968 the Conservative Shadow Defence Secretary Enoch Powell had made his notorious 'Rivers of Blood' speech, where he warned that 'in this country in 15 or 20 years' time the black man will have the whip hand over the white man'.[28] This speech and the bubbling up of fascism it signalled rocket-charged anti-racist organising in the UK, leading to the growth of grassroots groups such as the Southall Monitoring Group, the Asian Youth Movements, and the British Black Panthers which all monitored police activity and defended communities against brutality. In short, the 1981 Act sought to stop Enoch Powell's racist myth being realised, as people of colour rose up to fight back against racism.

The same questions around who could call themselves British, and who could live in Britain would continue to be asked over the decades that followed. Twenty years after the 1981 Nationality Act, as Britain marched into the new millennium, the country was experiencing a period of economic growth, and unemployment was at a 20-year low.[29] The booming economy meant that (sing along if you know the words by this point) the British government wanted more workers. Duly, the 2004 expansion of the European Union meant that people from the 'A10' countries (Cyprus, Czech Republic, Estonia, Hungary, Latvia, Lithuania, Malta, Poland, Slovakia and Slovenia) were able to come to the UK to live and work. According to the EU's website, this moment – the single largest expansion of the EU – indicated that 'The political divisions between east and west Europe are finally declared healed.' This loaded comment refers

---

28   www.telegraph.co.uk/comment/3643823/Enoch-Powells-Rivers-of-Blood-speech.html (last accessed 08/2020).

29   www.independent.co.uk/news/business/news/economic-boom-is-longest-in-uk-history-5372331.html (last accessed 08/2020).

to the fact that the majority of the A10 countries are former members of a collection of countries in Eastern Europe known as the 'Soviet Bloc' or 'Eastern bloc' which was created at the end of World War II.[30]

For many people from economically struggling former-Soviet countries, freedom of movement and the right to work in the UK, Ireland and Sweden opened up the door for new opportunities. According to estimates based on National Insurance Number applications, up to 500,000 people from the A10 countries came to work in the UK between 2004 and 2006.[31] However, a Bank of England report from 2007 estimates that as many as half of those people are likely to have returned to their origin country after six months or less.

What does 'intersectionality' mean for border-crossing?

In different ways, but much like other migration cohorts in Britain's history, people from Eastern Europe faced their own struggles and victories building lives in the UK. Migrant women in particular face oppression along intersecting axes – they experience xenophobia and misogyny, and these experiences are compounded for women who are also people of colour, queer, trans, disabled and working class. This is the idea underscoring 'intersectionality', a term coined by black feminist academic and lawyer Kimberlé Crenshaw. Her theory of intersectionality describes how the oppressions faced by, for example, a black

---

30   The Soviet Bloc was devised by Russia as a buffer zone of countries to protect it from any potential invasions from the 'Western Bloc' which was made up of the US and its Western European allies such as Britain.

31   David G. Blanchflower, Jumana Saleheen and Chris Shadforth, 'The Impact of the Recent Migration from Eastern Europe on the UK Economy,' External MPC Unit Discussion Paper No. 17, Bank of England (11 April 2007).

person who is also a trans woman crash together or 'intersect' to produce a particular experience which is different to that of a person who is cis, white or a man.

In the process of border-crossing, women wade through a series of stereotypes, prejudices and expectations based on who we are, where we come from, and our life choices. Sylwia Urbanska writing for the Green European Journal explains one way in which the experience of migration is highly gendered:

> Migrant parents who 'left their children behind' in Poland, and in particular migrant mothers, started to be seen after the mass outflow of 2004 as a new type of social deviant. Numerous politicians, priests, social workers, pedagogues, therapists, and lawyers expressed publicly the concern that the absence of the mother is dangerous for the health of affected children, but also a threat to families and to the reproduction of the nation. [. . .] It is interesting to note the class dimension of this 'moral panic', which stigmatises exclusively migrating from smaller cities or rural areas and spares more privileged migrants such as managers or 'Eurocrats'.[32]

Border-crossing can be incredibly difficult and dangerous – it seems very logical that a parent might leave a child to be cared for by support networks in their home country, and it is misogyny alone which breeds contempt for women who migrate without their children. However, parents also face criticism if they *do* migrate with their children. For example, as the cruel practice of separating children from their parents at the Mexican border has ramped up over the past few years, the acting director of US Immigration and Customs Enforcement (ICE) remarked that

---

32 www.greeneuropeanjournal.eu/on-the-move-experiences-of-migration-from-poland/ (last accessed 08/2020).

parents are 'ultimately the ones that are responsible for placing their children in this situation'. It seems that migrant parents cannot 'win' and are condemned whatever action they take.

While whiteness affords some Eastern European people a certain level of invisibility and palatability in Britain that people of colour can never access, the xenophobic treatment of white Eastern European people in Britain since 2004 is intrinsically connected to classism and racism. In his searing critique of the interrelation between racism and nationalism, *There Ain't No Black in the Union Jack*, British historian and academic Paul Gilroy describes 'new racism', which links together 'patriotism, nationalism, xenophobia, Englishness, Britishness, militarism and gender difference'.[33] Similarly, Sivanandan writing at the same time notes that xenophobia is:

> a racism that is not just directed at those with darker skins, from the former colonial territories, but at the newer categories of the displaced, the dispossessed and the uprooted, who are beating at western Europe's doors, the Europe that helped to displace them in the first place. It is a racism, that is, that cannot be colour-coded, directed as it is at poor whites as well [. . .] In the way it denigrates and reifies people before segregating and/or expelling them, it is a xenophobia that bears all the marks of the old racism.[34]

A. Sivanandan, Director of the Institute of Race Relations, articulates a key aspect of this 'new racism' or xenophobia: that it is primarily levelled at working-class people. The discrimination

---

33 P. Gilroy, *'There Ain't No Black in the Union Jack': The Cultural Politics of Race and Nation* (London: Hutchinson, 1987).

34 http://banmarchive.org.uk/articles/race&class/race&class%20Emergence%20 of%20xeno-racism.htm (last accessed 08/2020).

which white Eastern European people face when they come to Britain is forged in the fires of both xenophobia and classism.

Operation Nexus: a silent attack on EU migrants

This classism is particularly evident in the UK government's treatment of EU migrants through its shady Operation Nexus scheme. Operation Nexus is a joint operation between the police and Home Office which was supposed to target 'high harm' law-breakers, but in practice involves targeted deportations of homeless or rough-sleeping people to European Economic Area (EEA) countries. Guidance introduced by the Home Office in 2016 stated that a person from an EEA country who is rough-sleeping in the UK should not be allowed to stay in the country. According to current immigration law, people from the EEA who come to the UK to live and work are obliged to 'exercise their treaty rights' three months after arrival, which means being able to prove that you are either employed, looking for work, are a student or are 'self-sufficient'.[35] By stating that rough-sleeping was a breach of these treaty rights, the 2016 Home Office guidance gave immigration enforcement officers the powers to arrest, detain and deport rough-sleeping people from the EEA.

While the plain facts of this policy are concerning enough, the intricate details are even more sinister. A 2017 briefing by the Strategic Legal Fund noted that these targeted deportations had been devised as a solution to 'the steady increase in numbers of EEA nationals sleeping rough since 2011' and 'a persistent issue

---

35   This 'treaty' refers to the Citizens Rights Directive 2004/38/EC, sometimes referred to as the 'Free movement directive', which sets out the right to free movement for citizens of the EEA. The same treaty rights also apply to citizens of Switzerland even though it is not an EEA member.

with rough sleepers of Roma ethnicity in Westminster'.[36] Roma people[37] who are descended from North India and live mainly in Central and Eastern Europe face incredibly high levels of discrimination. The vast majority of Roma communities across Europe experience poverty,[38] high levels of unemployment and poor living conditions, as well as barriers to accessing public services such as health and social care and education. These conditions are a consequence of structural racism against Roma communities – from doctors who perpetuate stereotypical views about Roma women and their children and refuse to touch or treat them,[39] to inadequate town planning and a lack of roads and street lamps in Roma settlements. Given this context, it is particularly appalling that Roma people who come to the UK in search of a life-line are penalised for rough sleeping and face deportation from one of London's richest boroughs.

The saga surrounding this policy contains a further facet: it was revealed in 2017 that homeless charities St Mungo's and Thames Reach had collaborated with Operation Nexus. A report by Corporate Watch details how outreach workers from the charities conducted regular joint operations with Immigration Enforcement officers; in less than one year, 141 patrols led to the deportation of 127 people in Westminster alone.[40] During

---

36 www.luqmanithompson.com/wp-content/uploads/Operation-Nexus-Briefing-Paper.pdf (last accessed 08/2020).

37 Sometimes referred to as travellers, also referred to as gypsies, a term which some see as derogatory.

38 https://fra.europa.eu/en/news/2016/80-roma-are-risk-poverty-new-survey-finds (last accessed 08/2020).

39 Imkaan and UN Women 2018, '"A thousand ways to solve our problems": An analysis of existing Violence against Women and Girls (VAWG) approaches for minoritised women and girls in the Western Balkans and Turkey' (Istanbul: UN Women).

40 https://corporatewatch.org/the-round-up-rough-sleeper-immigration-raids-and-charity-collaboration-2/ (last accessed 08/2020).

my own volunteering stints at a Crisis homeless shelter, I would hear case-workers flippantly throwing around suggestions that staff should 'send back' rough-sleeping guests who were proving difficult to re-house. Conversely, I also worked alongside staff who refused to enter guests' immigration or nationality information into CHAIN, London's homelessness database, out of well-founded fear that data would be shared with the Home Office and used to detain and deport people. Human rights law organisations have been pushing back against Operation Nexus, including bringing a judicial review of the policy to the High Court, and bringing a case to the Court of Appeal that the Operation is unlawful.

The common experience of migrant communities throughout history and today, evidenced here, is that Britain systematically invites and exploits migrant labour, while at the same time making life untenable for anyone seeking (or struggling) to build a life here. This 'hot and cold' approach is encouraged and amplified across the political spectrum and in narratives spun by the media which we will further explore in Chapter 4. The thread which ties all of these events together – from slavery and colonisation, to the violence of the Partition of India and the systematic deportation of EU migrants – is that Britain's relationship to its borders tells a tale of inequality. Because of this, 'securing' Britain's borders is a further act of violence which shuts out people who cannot pay to negotiate their way around them. Migration is rarely a choice made lightly, but is often a survival strategy; sometimes a last resort or a life-line. The vast majority of people coming to the UK do not (as most of us do not) have a detailed knowledge of, for example, asylum seeking or how the welfare system works. For people who migrate to Britain, arriving on British soil brings a new set of challenges to add to, or replace the old.

Chapter 3

Why should migrants contribute?

'We are here because you were there.' – A. Sivanandan, Director of the Institute of Race Relations (1973–2013)

Dislike of difference is a learned trait in humans, not an ingrained sensibility. We have been spun centuries-old stories to convince us that walls, fences, borders, and cages are necessary, to separate us out from others who are different to us. We are told, even in the ninth richest country of the world, that this separation is necessary because resources are scarce. State-prescribed selfishness encourages us to fold in on ourselves. In the face of a public health crisis such as Covid-19, this leads people to stockpile food, toilet paper and hand sanitiser, knowing we can't trust the state to provide resources, and also pushing those who cannot stockpile into further danger. This obligatory individualism is the bedrock of an unequal society encouraged to be fearful of others, and to clutch our possessions close, as if they alone can save us.

Meritocracy myths and the 'resource drain' lie

Britain has been and continues to be one of the most powerful nations in the world. Because of this, people living in the UK are at the nucleus of the nerve centre, with the capital gathered from the global oppression of other people continuing to pour in – and finding its resting place in the bank accounts of the wealthy. Knowing this, the framing of migrant communities as a 'drain' on state resources is both racist and inaccurate. As a theory, it doesn't stack up, considering that economic forecasters calculated that people who came to the UK in 2016, for example, will make a net lifetime contribution of £26.9bn[1] to Britain's public finances. In practice, it is Britain that has historically done most of the 'draining' of resources from other countries.

In spite of this, migrant communities are commonly forced into a position of defending their existence in the UK on the basis of the fact that they 'contribute' to the economy. This line of argument is a house built on sand. Its jumping off point is the idea that people who are born and raised in Britain – and especially if they are white and wealthy – somehow *deserve* the spoils of the Empire: high quality education, a largely free health service and access to jobs,[2] while 'others' do not. Part of the problem here is how far the foundational myth of meritocracy is deeply embedded into the British psyche, thanks to a very successful ideological campaign which has been amplified by voices across the political spectrum.

Meritocracy works on the premise that anyone can acquire wealth and power (and should aspire to do so) if they work hard: we can all pull ourselves up by our bootstraps and become self-made folk if we put our nose to the grindstone. While this

---

1 https://assets.publishing.service.gov.uk/government/uploads/system/uploads/attachment_data/file/759376/The_Fiscal_Impact_of_Immigration_on_the_UK.pdf (last accessed 08/2020).

2 The unemployment rate for people over the age of 16 in the UK was 3.9 per cent as of August 2019 (Office of National Statistics). However, it is notable that this rate increases to 6.9 per cent for people of colour. (http://researchbriefings.files.parliament.uk/documents/SN06385/SN06385.pdf).

approach may reflect a minority of people's experiences, this way of thinking is fantastically divorced from the social realities of structural inequality along lines of class, race, disability, gender identity and more. These inequalities mean that some people will never acquire power and wealth, irrespective of how hard they work. Others might painstakingly edge a little closer to the top, dodging avalanches along the way, but doing twice the work to achieve half as much as people with more privilege.

Package meritocracy up with the capitalistic notion that there is something inherently good and noble about working, and you have the perfect stick with which to chastise working-class migrant communities. Capitalism tells us that work gives our lives ultimate value and meaning. Yet, under capitalism, being a content and healthy worker is a rare happy accident, not an intentional outcome. The first question a stranger might ask you on meeting, after your name, is: 'what do you do?'; we are encouraged through social rituals to measure each other by how we sell our labour. If we aren't working, then society tells us we should be 'job seeking', and if we're disabled or chronically sick then the government will obsessively assess, and reassess whether we are 'fit for work' The less we earn, and the less secure our job is, the more vulnerable to exploitation we become. If we can't afford to lose work, we are made to feel like we should be grateful to sell our labour to any buyer. This twisted logic suggests that the more we earn, the more important our lives are: this is evident in the fact that Boris Johnson got fast-tracked into intensive care when he contracted coronavirus, while people of colour working on the frontlines for the NHS have died in their masses.

The Covid-19 pandemic also exposed contradictions in the government's framing of some types of work as less important than others. In February 2020, Priti Patel announced a new set of post-Brexit immigration controls, which would categorise anyone earning under £25,000 as being 'low-skilled'. Some of these very same workers, including paramedics, radiographers and nurses – many of whom are migrants – were suddenly renamed 'key workers' in the face of an urgent health crisis. This shift in language is telling; it takes a global pandemic for the government to even slightly concede – in words only, not in any material change in working conditions – the value of a person beyond the salary they earn.

Contrary to this way of thinking, how 'hard' a person works and how much they contribute to any economy does not directly correlate to how comfortable their life is. While predominantly migrant workers in the gig economy complete 75-hour weeks on low wages without sick pay, holiday pay or pensions (a practice which is being challenged by trade unions),[3] the average high-flying CEO working the same hours or less is paid around £1.5k a week[4] alongside a benefits package such as private healthcare, a company car, corporate air travel and hefty retirement payouts. This learnt obsession with labour and toil, and quietly making the most of the hand you are dealt is what makes the idea that migrant communities need to 'work hard' to have their humanity recognised such a delicious confection for the British palate.

The idea that the value of a human being can be measured by their productivity is one of the vilest seductions of capitalism – the economic framework which governs much of the world. Capitalist nations work on the basis of a 'free market'. In a free market, prices for goods are decided by corpora-

---

3   United Voices of the World (UVW) and the Independent Workers of Great Britain (IWGB) unions, among others, lead campaigns to secure rights, in-house contracts and better wages for predominantly migrant workers in precarious jobs such as cleaning, security services, catering, private hire driving (including for Uber) and couriering.

4   www.independent.co.uk/news/business/news/the-30-best-and-worst-paid-jobs-in-the-uk-a6740731.html (last accessed 08/2020).

tions; accumulating private property and racking up profit are heavily encouraged, and the government takes a back seat. The natural fluctuations of the free market, according to supply and demand, is supposed to shake itself out so that consumers get the optimum version of what they want, when they want it. This is the idea of the free market operating as an 'invisible hand', gently pushing and pulling the right things into the right places and encouraging healthy competition to boost innovation. However, the evidence in front of us is that such a system is a hotbed for wealth inequality.

In his 2014 book *Capital in the Twenty-First Century*, the economist Thomas Piketty writes that a market economy based on private property is, 'if left to itself [. . .] potentially threatening to democratic societies and to the values of social justice'.[5] Kim Kelly, writing for *Teen Vogue* in 2018, puts forward a similar critique that capitalism is 'by nature, exploitative, and leads to a brutally divided society that tramples the working classes in favor of fattening the rich's wallets'.[6] Why does all of this matter? Because capitalism and the gaping wealth chasm in Britain[7] is inextricably linked to borders and migration.

We can only begin to meaningfully understand the complex web of migration experiences if we cast off capitalism-tinted glasses. The reason that politicians in the UK are so obsessed with migration is that it dovetails, in the popular imagination, with ideas about wealth and resources. This connection is actually valid, but not for the reasons that the finger-pointing

---

5   T. Piketty, *Capital In the Twenty-First Century* (Cambridge, MA: Harvard University Press, 2014).

6   www.teenvogue.com/story/what-capitalism-is (last accessed 08/2020).

7   According to a 2017 report by the Organisation for Economic Co-operation and Development (OECD), the highest levels of income inequality in Europe are reached in the United Kingdom and the Baltic States: www.oecd.org/els/soc/cope-divide-europe-2017-background-report.pdf (last accessed 08/2020).

news headlines would have us believe. In Eric Williams' 1944 book *Capitalism & Slavery*, he puts forward a well-evidenced argument that transatlantic slavery and the forced labour of millions of African people played a key role in providing the basis for the industrial revolution which made Britain wealthy. Williams writes that many of the British banks established in the eighteenth century were directly associated with the slave trade, and that Lloyd's bank, for example, was founded in 1765 and flourished through insuring slave ships.[8] Similarly, David and Alexander Barclay who were personally engaged in the slave trade were also members of the Quaker family which co-founded Barclays, which financed plantation mortgages.[9] Furthermore, capital from the slave trade funded the growth of metallurgical industries and the development of the first steam engine. This reality casts a different light on the question of who, historically, has 'contributed' to the UK economy.

If we flip the gaze back on *Britain* as a drain on resources in the Global South, a different narrative emerges. Guyanese historian and activist Walter Rodney's 1972 book *How Europe Underdeveloped Africa* makes the case that European depopulation and depression of the African continent during transatlantic slavery and colonial projects has left a devastating socioeconomic legacy. The impacts of the forced removal of 12.5 million people from Africa to North America, the Caribbean and South America (only 10.7 million of whom survived the journey)[10] directly relates to the continued economic status of these regions. In a speech in 2016, Obama stated that 'despite significant growth in much of the continent, Africa's entire GDP is still only about the

---

8   www.bbc.co.uk/history/british/abolition/building_britain_gallery_02.shtml (last accessed 08/2020).

9   www.ucl.ac.uk/lbs/person/view/2146643749 (last accessed 08/2020).

10 www.slavevoyages.org/ (last accessed 08/2020).

GDP of France',[11] a startling comparison considering that South Africa alone (just one of the 55 countries that make up Africa) is two times bigger than France.

The stain and shame of colonial legacies

Sivanandan's aphorism 'we are here because you were there' is a succinct explanation of what happened when imperial Britain began marauding around the world half a century ago, murdering, terrorising and enslaving populations, stealing resources, gutting economies, and disrupting governance and infrastructure. It should come as no surprise that people living in colonies and former colonies would seek to retrace the well-worn paths carved by European colonisers and find themselves on Britain's shores, intrigued for a taste of the alleged greatness of Britain which has been used as both a mystical carrot, and a stick to beat people for centuries.

The legacy of colonial rule and ruin is long-lasting and ongoing. Not only has Britain failed to meaningfully recognise the impact of its colonial history – in 2013, then Foreign Secretary William Hague stood up in the House of Commons and announced that 'We continue to deny liability on behalf of the Government [. . .] for the actions of the colonial administration'[12] – the notable absence of colonialism from the British school curriculum maintains a huge knowledge gap about this era of history. A 2014 YouGov poll revealed some uncomfortable truths: 59 per cent of British people are proud of the British Empire (compared to 19

11 www.independent.co.uk/news/world/africa/is-the-entire-gdp-of-africa-really-just-equal-to-that-of-france-a7367906.html (last accessed 08/2020).

12 www.gov.uk/government/news/statement-to-parliament-on-settlement-of-mau-mau-claims (last accessed 08/2020).

per cent who think Britain should be ashamed of the Empire).[13] 49 per cent of people think that former colonies are 'better off' for being colonised, and a third of respondents would welcome back the Empire with open arms.

Britain's inability to grapple with its colonial past goes some way to explaining why borders are seen as benign, inevitable and necessary. Borders are not generally understood to be weapons of the state; the harassment and exclusion of people using border enforcement is perceived by many people as normal. This status quo – accepting that our ability to 'belong' is decided by the government – is the result of a convincing centuries-long propaganda exercise. Living across and beyond borders is infinitely more powerful, more human, more open, more creative and more compassionate than the narrow restrictions and limitations that immigration policy will allow. Yet, contemporary narratives around citizenship seem to draw a clear distinction between who is and isn't British, and in the process of this myth-making, there are powerful forces at play.

---

13 http://cdn.yougov.com/cumulus_uploads/document/6quatmbimd/Internal_Results_140725_Commonwealth_Empire-W.pdf (last accessed 08/2020).

Chapter 4

Building borders through headlines and column inches

'Much of the media cares less about painting a full picture; it's all about throwing anything, mostly shit, Pollock-like at a canvas and hoping it sticks.' – Moya Lothian-McLean, *gal-dem*

It seems that the more politicians and pundits talk about borders and security, the more anxieties are heightened about a 'need' for more security. From the fourteenth century father of Protestantism Martin Luther, who in his writings referred to Jewish people as 'devils incarnate', to Conservative MP Peter Griffiths' winning 1964 election slogan: 'If you want a n*gger for a neighbour, vote Labour', power-seeking white men have used the mythology of undesirable outsiders as a device to win (racist) hearts and minds. However, these kinds of messages only work because the stage has been set for them to be well-received. People aren't born with racist thoughts, and don't just wake up one day with a beating heart of xenophobia. A delicate alchemy of privilege and the deep, historical imbuing of racism into huge structures like the job market and the criminal justice system, as well as sectors such as politics, entertainment and education, all stack up to create racist realities (which exist whether you 'see' race or not). These ideas and realities proliferate through a racist media industry – which in turn upholds the border nation.

The British media plays a significant role in building borders: the way that stories are told about borders and who deserves to be a citizen creates accepted 'truths' about migrant communities. News coverage in 2015 relating to the case of East London schoolgirl Shamima Begum, for example, provides a pertinent illustration of the convergence of racism, sexism and Islamophobia which leads to a British child's citizenship being revoked. After being groomed online, 15-year-old Shamima Begum left East London, crossed borders and joined the Islamic State in Syria. A week after her arrival she was married to an ISIS fighter, and in the four years that followed she gave birth to three children. After being found in a Syrian refugee camp in 2019 and asking to return to Britain, Begum's British citizenship was revoked by the UK Home Office.

Headlines in national publications at the time, including the *Telegraph*, *Independent* and *Sky News*, variously referred to Begum as a 'jihadi bride', an 'ISIS bride' and a 'pregnant IS teen'. This victim-blaming language overlooks Begum's inability to consent to a marriage ceremony at 15 under UK law, and consciously ignores the fact that she is likely a survivor of grooming and statutory rape. For communities of colour, this strategic process of 'othering' attempts to destabilise our right to reside, and in the most violent cases, seeks to undermine our humanity. The mainstream media's role in shaping public opinion cannot be overstated. Public opinion works to steer the decision-making of a government desperate to stay relevant and in power.

The pale, stale media industry

The unbearable whiteness of media has a profound impact on the content that is available for us to consume, from newspapers and documentaries to TV news, books, podcasts and radio shows. In the UK, the media industry is 94 per cent white[1] and incredibly monocultural; for example, less than 0.5 per cent of journalists in the UK are Muslim.[2] This creates a situation where the tone and lean of narratives around 'Britishness' and who can belong are set by people who have likely never experienced the violence of borders, and whose experiences of crossing them are characterised by breezing through security with a wave of their passport en route to skiing holidays, gap years and destination weddings.

In turn, this means that unless we as media consumers have the critical lens, time and resources to go digging around for more information from a wider range of perspectives (and even when we do), we are susceptible to building ideas about the world we live in that are based upon a very narrow viewpoint. Due to the whiteness of media, the euro-centricity of the school curriculum, and the general denial of racism and privilege which underpins inequality in the UK, this viewpoint is unlikely to have a grasp of how Britain's colonial exploits set the stage for border-crossing. Mainstream media also fails to recognise how structural racism continues the colonial project in the present day. Rather than news stories about migration being reported and critiqued by people who have an informed or lived understanding of the issue, the terms of the debate are set by people reclining on the most privileged peaks of society. These terms, which in the past decade in particular have been largely racist, exclusionary and dehumanising, have quickly caught on the kindling of genuine economic damage caused by ten years of austerity in Britain, and spread like wildfire.

---

1 www.theguardian.com/media-network/2016/mar/24/british-journalism-diversity-white-female-male-survey (last accessed 08/2020).

2 www.independent.co.uk/voices/why-the-british-media-is-responsible-for-the-rise-in-islamophobia-in-britain-a6967546.html (last accessed 08/2020).

An attack on working-class solidarity

Much of the anti-migrant rhetoric I hear in conversations and see online – including by people who migrated to the UK only a few decades ago – is scripted straight from the playbook of news headlines. Concerns that, for example, EU migrants are 'taking' jobs, housing, public services and welfare support are commonly articulated using very similar and specific phrases: 'benefit fraud', 'health tourism' and worries about Britain's 'sovereignty'. When deployed so relentlessly on the front pages of national newspapers, this messaging hits home because it nurtures seeds that were planted long ago. The British news machine has been pumping out stories about so-called 'benefit fraud' for over a decade, roughly in line with when the government started devising threatening campaigns and legislation reforms targeted at tackling benefit 'theft'. Adding migrant communities to the mix is simply a new twist on an old recipe; a cunning 'divide and rule' tactic which seeks to hack away at solidarity across class and race lines. By separating working class and migrant communities into the 'deserving' and 'undeserving', citizens and non-citizens, the fraudulent and the honest, a giant gulf emerges.

The far-right racist UK Independence Party (UKIP) found root in this gulf, gathering steam after Nigel Farage became the leader of the party in 2006. UKIP's primary campaign objective involved seeking to get Britain out of the EU by pitting the 'white working class' against migrant communities, as if the two groups are separable and distinct. The confection of the 'white working class' is a contradiction in terms, considering that migrant communities are disproportionately working class, and that people of colour in the UK are more likely to be in precarious and low-paid work, or unemployed, in comparison to their

53

white counterparts.[3] UKIP's whitewashed little Britain fantasy conveniently glosses over the fact that throughout history, communities of colour have stood shoulder to shoulder with white comrades against our shared adversary: bosses seeking to exploit our labour.

From the Grunwick Strike in the 1970s, when the formidable Jayaben Desai led South Asian women workers at a film processing factory to strike against poor conditions, to numerous hunger strikes over the past decade in Yarl's Wood Immigration Removal Centre where migrant women work for £1 an hour, migrant communities and people of colour have also been at the sharp edge of working class oppression. As one woman recounted on *Detained Voices*, which publishes verbatim statements from people incarcerated in UK immigration detention centres:

> They are using us to work for £1. Most of [the people in detention] are coming from prison because they are working illegally. So now the immigration removal prisons are using us to do the laundry, to cook, to wash. The working conditions are really bad. In the kitchen we cook the food, washing the plates for £1 per hour. Too many girls don't want to do it but we have no choice. It's threatening behaviour.[4]

It's plain that UKIP's whitewashed vision for Britain is a backwards fascistic fairytale: the decline of the party is to be welcomed, and working class communities continue to be more 'diverse' than any other social class. For a party who only ever put one MP in parliament (albeit, while also winning 24 seats

---

3   www.tuc.org.uk/sites/default/files/LivingontheMargins.pdf (last accessed 08/2020).

4   https://detainedvoices.com/2015/10/07/they-are-using-us-to-work-for-1/ (last accessed 08/2020).

in the European parliament), UKIP managed to hold considerable court in the political sphere. The party's rising popularity dragged all parties to the political right, as they scrambled to show that they too could be 'tough on immigration'. In the run-up to the 2015 election, the Labour party released a much criticised piece of merchandise: a garish red mug emblazoned with the slogan 'Controls on immigration: I'm voting Labour'. The Conservatives also panicked that UKIP was going to win over a chunk of the electorate, and in a desperate last-ditch plea, promised a referendum on leaving the EU if they won a majority, which, somehow, they managed to do.

This context leads us into a current moment where media discourse on migration has become a putrefied emulsion of all out guns-blazing racism, suspended in the festering slop which is capitalism, dashing away humanity in favour of the balance sheet. Questions of objectivity, 'healthy discussion' or presenting 'both sides' on the topic of migration are at this point obsolete. Politicans across the spectrum – including neoliberal careerists on the British left – are guilty of failing to hold the line when it comes to updholding the basic human right to move. For example, in summer 2020 a record number of people tried to cross the English channel from France, seeking safety in the UK. In response, Home Secretary Priti Patel called on France to intercept boats and return them, overlooking the fact that people were being forced to take more dangerous routes in response to the UK border being further galvanised in Northern France. Labour leader Keir Starmer was notably silent on the issue, presumably continuing to court public support at all costs, as he did a few months prior when he called Black Lives Matter a 'moment' not a 'movement'.[5] The scale of human lives snatched

---

5   https://twitter.com/BBCBreakfast/status/1277556165040148485 (last accessed 08/2020).

away at Britain's borders – whether in the freezing cold sea, in high security detention centres, or on migration routes made treacherous by strict immigration laws – is devastating. We are beyond an exercise where factors can be balanced, and the 'pros' and 'cons' carefully weighed.

The dehumanising language of the refugee crisis

Words and language play a huge role in the media-fuelled anti-migrant campaign. Words can be distilled down to their literal dictionary definition, but they also carry connotations of all the personal, cultural and emotional meanings we heap onto them. Words do not drop from the sky as divine descriptors, but they are created in society. In short: words have meanings. Words conjure particular thoughts, feelings and associations. When far-right commentator Katie Hopkins writes a stream of racist vitriol for the *Sun* in 2015, it has the effect of dehumanising migrant communities and facilitating the murder and deaths of people migrating, leaving blood on her hands.

No, I don't care. Show me pictures of coffins, show me bodies floating in water, play violins and show me skinny people looking sad. I still don't care. [. . .] Some of our towns are festering sores, plagued by swarms of migrants and asylum seekers, shelling out benefits like Monopoly money. Make no mistake, these migrants are like cockroaches. They might look a bit 'Bob Geldof's Ethiopia circa 1984', but they are built to survive a nuclear bomb. They are survivors. – Katie Hopkins, 17 April 2015 the *Sun*

Hopkins' column outlines her reflections on what was dubbed by national and international media at the time as the 'migrant crisis' or 'refugee crisis': an intensified period of fatalities during attempts to cross the Mediterranean Sea, journeys which were compounded by British military intervention. During the second year of the crisis, an estimated 362,000 people[6] embarked on treacherous journeys across the Mediterranean, with many people fleeing conflicts in Syria, Afghanistan and Iraq. Since 2015, each year 2,500–5,000 people have been reported dead or missing after attempting to make the crossing.[7] According to records kept by Dutch NGO, United for Cultural Action, 27,000 people have drowned trying to cross the Mediterranean since 1993.[8] I present these figures to give a sense of the scale of the issue; they provide context to the national shame of Britain's hostile response to the crisis.

By March 2019, Britain had resettled only 15,000 of the 6.7 million people fleeing conflict in Syria,[9] around 4.6 million of whom are being hosted in Syria's neighbouring countries – Lebanon, Jordan and Turkey.[10] This lack of British humanitarian assistance, as a bare minimum, is particularly galling because the conflicts that are pushing people to uproot their families and make life-threatening journeys are directly related to British military intervention. The increase in attempted migrations across the Mediterranean can be tracked back to a key milestone in 2011, when NATO (a military alliance of 29 countries), led by the UK and France, began a military assault of air strikes on Libya in order to overthrow the Libyan dictator Muammar Gaddafi. In the first few days of bombing, between 60–90 people were

---

6   www.unhcr.org/uk/europe-emergency.html (last accessed 08/2020).

7   https://data2.unhcr.org/en/situations/mediterranean (last accessed 08/2020).

8   www.theguardian.com/world/2018/jun/20/the-list-europe-migrant-bodycount (last accessed 08/2020).

9   https://commonslibrary.parliament.uk/insights/migration-statistics-how-many-asylum-seekers-and-refugees-are-there-in-the-uk/ (last accessed 08/2020).

10   www.jstor.org/stable/10.7864/j.ctt1c2cqws (last accessed 08/2020).

killed. A few months later Gaddafi was captured and killed, but the airstrikes continued, resulting in at least 478 and possibly up to 737 civilian deaths by 2019.[11] The power vacuum which emerged after Gaddafi's death has transformed Libya into the gateway for migration from the African continent – North and West Africa in particular – into Europe. Due to its northern position and un-managed coastline, Libya provides a departure point for people who are headed to Turkey, Greece or Italy.

Given this context, Hopkins – whose main motivation seems to be making a quick buck as a vapid vessel for populist racism – demonstrates a purposeful lack of compassion for people caught up in the migrant crisis. A mere two months after the *Sun* article was published, in July 2015, the newly-elected Prime Minister David Cameron appears on ITV News and directly parrots the *Sun*'s rhetoric, warning of a 'swarm of people coming across the Mediterranean [. . .] wanting to come to Britain because Britain has got jobs'. The impact of this coordinated and repeated language – essentially comparing people to insects and infestations by referring to them as 'swarms' and 'cockroaches' is incredibly dehumanising. As rapper and writer Akala explains on a TV panel show in the same year:

> We're leaving people fleeing [. . .] conflict to drown in the sea, while giving a woman space in a national newspaper to refer to them as cockroaches. And when you refer to humans as cockroaches, that is a mandate for murder. Let's be clear about that. The moment human beings become non-human that is

11 According to credible news reports aggregated by New America, www.newamerica.org/in-depth/americas-counterterrorism-wars/airstrikes-and-civilian-casualties-libya/ (last accessed 08/2020).

a mandate for murder, and there is a long historical parallel for that.[12]

Words that oppress and images that kill

Akala's comments make reference to the leveraging of dehumanising language by oppressive, racist and xenophobic regimes throughout history. 'Scientific' racism gathered steam in Europe in the eighteenth and nineteenth century, creating a fictional hierarchy of races with white people at the top and black people at the bottom – in close proximity to animals, which leads to the racist comparison of black people to monkeys. These concepts are alive in the present day: in 2018, Australia's *Herald Sun* published a cartoon depicting record-breaking tennis champion Serena Williams as an angry ape, and in 2019, a BBC radio presenter was fired after tweeting a picture comparing Meghan Markle's baby to a monkey.[13] These ideas are part of a trajectory which includes the mass genocide and enslavement of African people during the transatlantic slave trade.

The slave trade was propped up by the popularising of racist ideas and images of black people, including the racist concept of the muscular, violent and sexually predatory 'black buck' caricature (buck meaning a male horned animal). This caricature was used and continues to be used to justify hypersexualising and brutalising black men indiscriminately – such as 14-year old Emmett Till, who was lynched in 1955 after a white woman accused him of whistling at her (only to retract her claim many decades later). Similarly, the dehumanising hyper-sexualisation

---

12   www.youtube.com/watch?v=7YCu5B6AMoQ (last accessed 08/2020).

13   www.indiatoday.in/lifestyle/celebrity/story/bbc-fires-presenter-for-tweeting-racist-pic-comparing-meghan-markle-and-harry-s-baby-boy-to-monkey-1521568-2019-05-10 (last accessed 08/2020).

of black women was used to justify their systematic rape by slave owners which also manifests in our abuse in the present day: in a study by UK-based charity Imkaan, black women remarked that their experiences of racialised sexual harassment include men assuming that they are 'fair game' and 'up for it'.[14]

These same tropes – comparing people of colour to animals – continues to be deployed and utilised against marginalised and oppressed communities. In a 1983 Israeli parliament committee, Rafael Eytan, the former Israeli chief of staff referred to Palestinians as 'drugged cockroaches in a bottle', and in 2014 Ayelet Shaked who was later appointed Israel's Minister for Justice, in a Facebook post called for the slaughter of Palestinian children, who she called 'little snakes'.[15] Social media and tech giants such as Facebook are key stakeholders in this landscape of division and hatred; their huge platforms act as international news outlets, enabling information – including offensive, fascistic content – to be circulated with ease to their 2.45 billion users. Despite having a user base which is almost double the population of China, Facebook consistently pushes back against the kind of regulation that other news platforms, and even entire countries are forced to adhere to. Speaking at the Anti-Defamation League's summit on antisemitism and hate in New York in November 2019, actor and screenwriter Sacha Baron Cohen said (on Facebook's 'apolitical' running of bigoted political adverts):

> If you pay them, Facebook will run any 'political' ad you want, even if it's a lie. And, they'll even help you micro-target those lies to their users for maximum effect. Under this twisted logic, if Facebook were around in the 1930s, it would have

14   www.youtube.com/watch?v=lJ-qpvibpdU (last accessed 08/2020).

15   https://electronicintifada.net/blogs/ali-abunimah/israeli-lawmakers-call-genocide-palestinians-gets-thousands-facebook-likes (last accessed 08/2020).

allowed Hitler to post 30-second ads on his 'solution' to the 'Jewish problem'.

These images and comparisons have the impact of dehumanising people of colour, migrant communities, and marginalised ethno-cultural groups, providing justification for abuse, exploitation and genocide. Similarly, Trump describes Mexican people migrating to the US as 'animals'[16] who will 'infest our Country'[17] and posts on Instagram, referencing the US-Mexico border: 'You know why you can enjoy a day at the zoo? Because walls work'. When I spoke with a genocide scholar during a training course for campaigners in 2017, they told me that the rhetoric of US President Donald Trump was a genocidal tactic which paved the way for mass murder.

These examples show the direct link between the proliferation of racist ideas and images, and the exclusion, oppression, and killing of groups of people through the creation of physical, ideological and legal borders within society. The racist rhetoric spewed by world leaders is amplified and mimicked by media messaging. This has a powerful impact on how society views migrant communities, which in turn steers government rhetoric, policies and immigration laws as parties frantically compete to dance most exuberantly to the beat of their perception of the electorate.

Individual stories can't paint a complete picture

This very same dehumanisation, propagated by the media, fed the locomotive which propelled Britain into Brexit. The UK

---

16   https://eu.usatoday.com/story/news/politics/2018/05/16/trump-immigrants-animals-mexico-democrats-sanctuary-cities/617252002/ (last accessed 08/2020).
17   https://twitter.com/realDonaldTrump/status/1009071403918864385? (last accessed 08/2020).

media's approach to storytelling, from its focus on single 'human stories' to its gleeful propagation of clickbait racist narratives, fails to properly interrogate the structural inequality which underpins border violence. As anti-migrant discourse reached fever pitch in 2015 when Cameron described people fleeing a conflict Britain is implicated in as a 'swarm', a series of high-profile news stories coalesced to set a new tone and tenor for discussions around migration. In different ways, these stories – which I'll explore below – demonstrate how the hardening of Britain's borders which followed via Brexit was both a symptom of and response to relentless anti-migrant sentiment. This all-out xenophobia, rooted in centuries of racist concepts which have a stronghold on the European collective imagination, was sustained even in the face of horrific tragedy and loss of life.

Firstly: the circulation of a single photo starkly depicted the human cost of the UK's small island imperialism. In September 2015, three year old Alan Shenu (named in media reports by Turkish authorities as Aylan Kurdi) boarded a small over-crowded rubber dinghy with his parents and brother in Bodrum, on the south-east coast of Turkey. The family were from Kobani in Northern Syria, and were fleeing vicious conflict whipped up by the Islamic State. The dinghy was headed for the Greek island of Kos, which like the islands of Lesbos and Samos had become key destinations for people seeking to travel from Turkey to seek asylum in Europe. A few minutes after boarding, the dinghy was capsized by a large wave, causing Alan, his mother and brother to be thrown into the sea and drown.

Alan's body was discovered by Turkish police early the next morning, washed up on a beach. The little boy's body was photographed by journalists and quickly went viral; in the photographs he is dressed in shorts, trainers and a red T-shirt, lying on his front with his face turned to one side, almost as if sleeping peacefully. As messages of rage and condolences shared using the hashtag #KiyiyaVuranInsanlik ('humanity washed ashore') began to amass online, it was too late both for Alan, and for the conservative toll of around 250,000 people who had already died in the four preceding years of conflict.[18]

Research carried out in 2017 into the 'empathic response to humanitarian disasters'[19] showed that in the wake of the photograph's publication, there was a considerable spike in donations to humanitarian efforts, and increased Google searches for the terms 'Syria' and 'refugees'. The researchers refer to Alan as the 'identified individual victim'; a conduit which enables people who may feel unaffected by a particular tragedy, conflict or disaster to relate to it and feel empathy. Another example of the identified individual victim is 15-year-old Anne Frank, author of *The Diary of Anne Frank*, which became for many people who weren't directly affected by the holocaust a vehicle through which to empathise with victims and survivors. This framing can feel unpleasant: the idea that some (in fact, many) people need to be able to conjure up the feeling of being directly affected to feel concern about genocide should not sit well with us.

While Alan's death was both an individual tragedy, and an example of a wider humanitarian issue, the issue of global and structural inequality which would lay the finger of blame on Europe itself did not 'cut through' the media noise around this one family's tragedy. This meant that people consuming the news were able to comprehend Alan's death as an anomaly; an aberration in an otherwise functioning border system. Once the images disappeared from newspaper front pages, people who weren't directly affected by the Syrian war were able to go about their day.

---

18   www.pnas.org/content/114/4/640 (last accessed 08/2020).
19   Ibid.

A mere five weeks after Alan's death, donations dropped from their 100-fold increase back to their starting position. The question remaining for Alan's family and loved ones was: would the outpouring of empathy have a real-time impact on the restrictive border enforcement which led up to Alan's death? The answer is: it did not. The research report concludes: 'After a string of boat disasters claimed 2,510 lives between January and May, and put year 2016 on course to be the deadliest ever for refugees, Alan's father said that 'my Aylan died for nothing'.

White feminism joins forces with the far right

Three months later, the media gaze shifts to another incident, this time a little closer to Britain's shores, in the German city of Cologne. A spate of racist media coverage brought attention to a series of sexual assaults, which according to a widely quoted leaked document, were perpetrated against over 1,200 women on New Years Eve in 2015. The Cologne police chief stated at the time that the perpetrators were men of 'Arab or North African appearance'. An in-depth investigation by journalists Yermi Brenner and Katrin Ohlendorf who analysed official reports and media coverage, as well as interviewing authorities, survivors and witnesses, revealed inaccuracies in the police report, including suggesting that the figure is closer to a few dozen assaults,[20] and that a small number of perpetrators were formally identified meaning their ethnicities are unclear. Brenner and Ohlendorf's investigation doesn't seek to invalidate the very real experiences of survivors, which must always be believed, but instead invites us to ask questions about how the media contorts

20   https://thecorrespondent.com/4401/time-for-the-facts-what-do-we-know-about-cologne-four-months-later/1073698080444-e20ada1b (last accessed 08/2020).

an incident to fit within sensationalist racist narratives in order to sell newspapers.

For many feminists adhering to the neoliberal brand of white feminism, the Cologne sexual assaults were difficult incidents to navigate. This moment exposed the flawed, simplistic understanding which positions people who cross borders or seek asylum as helpless victims. An intersectional feminist lens, in contrast, works from a starting point of complexity – knowing that oppression along different lines such as race, gender, and immigration status can crash together and 'intersect' to produce complicated and varied experiences. We know first-hand that people of colour within our communities can be perpetrators of sexual violence while also experiencing racism and state violence themselves. Men can live under and benefit from cisgender heteropatriarchy, while at the same time being oppressed by racism and border violence. This does not mean we should excuse or ignore any incident or pattern of sexual violence, and we also cannot condone racism and immigration enforcement action as a response to sexism and misogyny. One oppression does not cancel out the other.

Of course, the response by the European press and political elites was overtly racist and failed to address the long-term needs of survivors. Rather than leveraging this spate of assaults to, for example, place a duty on schools to provide compulsory lessons for all students on consent, rape culture, and harmful gender stereotypes, and better fund rape crisis centres to support victims, in July 2016 the German government instead passed laws making it easier to deport people who had committed sexual assault. While on the surface this new law may have provided temporary solace to survivors, in fact it leads us down a dangerous path – leveraging border controls as a form of punishment rather than actually addressing gender inequality as the root cause and consequence of sexual violence globally.

This framing of men of colour as being *inherently* sexually violent, which is underpinned by an agenda to demonise, criminalise and exclude migrant men specifically and migrant communities in general, has impacts that expand beyond individual perpetrators. For example, when as people from migrant communities, or people of colour, we experience sexual violence within our communities, we are often forced to make a (non-) choice between disclosing abuse and thus feeding the fire of racist sentiment, and keeping silent. As feminist activist Huda Jawad writes in 2019:

> Muslim women survivors are forced to reckon with the discomfort of feeling like they are 'flogging' their trauma to their community's oppressor in order to be heard at all. Is it any wonder that for many Muslim women, the stakes of saying #MeToo are simply too high and the possibility of support or healing is minimal?[21]

In the example of Cologne, the media messaging provided easy fuel to anti-migrant agendas, which in turn set the stage for anti-migrant law-making (in Europe and beyond), and galvanised the border state. To give a few examples: in January 2016 the *Telegraph* ran an editorial with the sub-head 'How long before the women of Cologne are advised to stay indoors, or even cover their heads?',[22] the *New York Post* ran an article with the headline 'Germans clash over "rapefugees" who carried out

---

21   B. Fileborn and R. Loney-Howes, *#MeToo and the Politics of Social Change* (London: Palgrave Macmillan, 2019).

22   www.telegraph.co.uk/news/worldnews/europe/germany/12087780/Cologne-assault-Cultural-difference-is-no-excuse-for-rape.html (last accessed 08/2020).

mass sex attack,'[23] and in a speech at Youngstown State University, Donald Trump cited the attacks as a reason to clamp down on immigration to the US, setting the scene for the abhorrent 'Muslim travel ban' he would implement in 2017. He stated: 'you know what a disaster this massive immigration has been to Germany and the people of Germany – crime has risen to levels that no one thought they would ever see'.[24] The xenophobia and Islamophobia inherent in these ideas are overt. The baseless fear of other legal systems being imported to the UK, resulting in for example, women being forced to wear hijabs, are tired cliches from the racist playbook, and simply use real Muslim women's lives as fodder in a point-scoring exercise. Nonetheless, these ideas are powerful and have taken root in the popular imagination: research by Hope not Hate revealed that a third of British people actually believe (erroneously) that there are areas of the UK governed by sharia law.[25]

This pervasive xenophobia explains why, across the channel, British politicians also weighed in with problematic positions on the Cologne sexual assaults. Speaking on BBC Question Time in 2017, Labour MP for Birmingham Yardley, Jess Phillips, said: 'a very similar situation to what happened in Cologne could be described on Broad Street in Birmingham every week where women are baited and heckled'. Writing for *Media Diversified* in 2018, Nadya Ali explains how Phillips' comments slot neatly into the messy tradition of white feminism:

23 https://nypost.com/2016/01/10/germans-slam-rapefugees-in-wake-of-mass-sexual-attack/ (last accessed 08/2020).

24 https://businessjournaldaily.com/read-transcript-of-trumps-speech-at-ysu/ (last accessed 08/2020).

25 www.independent.co.uk/news/uk/home-news/uk-no-go-zones-muslim-sharia-law-third-poll-hope-not-hate-far-right-economic-inequality-a8588226.html (last accessed 08/2020).

What [Phillips] said in full was, 'We have to attack what we perceive as being patriarchal culture coming into any culture that isn't patriarchal and making sure we tell people not to be like that.' Does she consider the UK to be a non-patriarchal culture? I think she does. [Phillips continues] 'But we should be careful in this country before we rest on our laurels when two women are murdered every week in this country.' Those must be non-patriarchal laurels to which she refers.[26]

These same dehumanising racist 'panic buttons' were activated by a third high-profile news story back in the mid 2010s. Child abuse rings which had been operating without social services intervening for over two decades in the North of England – including in around Rotherham and Rochdale – were exposed, and described as the 'biggest child protection scandal in UK history'.[27] Court records show that of the 56 men convicted of grooming and sexual offences against girls in the region, 53 were Asian, 50 were Muslim, and three were white, despite most sexual offenders in the UK being white men.[28] This led to a frenzy of media reporting and the proliferation of sensationalised narratives which cooked up and fleshed out the idea that there is something inherent in these men of colour which had led them to abuse white girls specifically. The border regime, therefore, could provide a solution: the abusers were threatened with deportation to Pakistan after judges upheld a decision to strip them of their British citizenship.

---

26   https://mediadiversified.org/2018/02/06/jess-phillips-lena-dunham-and-white-feminism/ (last accessed 08/2020).

27   A. Gladman and A. Heal, *Child Sexual Exploitation After Rotherham* (London: Jessica Kingsley Publisher, 2017).

28   www.rotherham.gov.uk/downloads/file/279/independent-inquiry-into-child-sexual-exploitation-in-rotherham (last accessed 08/2020).

As always, the details of these heinous patterns of abuse are a bit more complicated than can be squeezed into a *Daily Mail* headline. In contradiction to the popular narrative (of Asian men abusing white girls), the 2014 Independent Inquiry into Child Sexual Abuse revealed that British Asian girls had also been the targets of the child sexual exploitation rings, but that this demographic group was less likely to report abuse to the authorities. Writing for the *Guardian* in 2013, Alexandra Topping remarks that British Asian girls experiencing sexual exploitation are being 'missed by the authorities because agencies are too focused on a model of grooming involving white victims'.[29] Of course, these nuances were absent in media reporting of these cases. As in the case of the Cologne attacks, rather than focusing on the needs of the survivors and the services which should have been supporting them, broad generalisations were made about Muslim men and Muslim communities in general, and used to further embed a narrative of division which could be used to justify building up borders.

In August 2017 Sarah Champion, MP for Rotherham and at the time Shadow Secretary of State for Women and Equalities, published a column in the *Sun* with the headline 'British Pakistani men ARE raping and exploiting white girls. . .and it's time we faced up to it.'[30] The article begins: 'Britain has a problem with British Pakistani men raping and exploiting white girls. There. I said it. Does that make me a racist? [. . .] These people are predators and the common denominator is their ethnic heritage.' Champion's words have meaning. In March 2019, a white supremacist, Brenton Tarrant carried out two horrific terrorist attacks at a mosque in Christchurch in New Zealand

29   www.theguardian.com/society/2013/sep/10/abuse-asian-girls-missed-white-victims (last accessed 08/2020).

30   www.thesun.co.uk/news/4218648/british-pakistani-men-raping-exploiting-white-girls/ (last accessed 08/2020).

during Friday prayer, resulting in the deaths of 51 people. Tarrant wrote in white paint on one of the ammo clips he used in the massacre: 'for Rotherham'. Tarrant's own agency in perpetrating the violent actions he did should not be remotely underestimated – at the same time, by peddling narratives which brand entire groups with the actions of individuals, politicians pave the way for a spectrum of violence which includes terrorism and massacre.

Terrorism and white supremacy

It seems that whenever men of colour and migrant men are violent, their violence is attributed to an inherent difference and non-Britishness; to their blackness, or their Muslim-ness. However, when white men are violent, media outlets are quick to perform the most elaborate mental acrobatics to create three-dimensional narratives for their actions. For example, white supremacist Dylann Roof who shot dead nine African American people during a Bible study group in 2015 in the hopes of starting a 'race war' was not only taken to Burger King after being arrested, but was described by the *LA Times*[31] and *Washington Post*[32] as a 'lone wolf'. Similarly, far-right terrorist Anders Breivik, who killed 77 people in Norway in 2011 (69 people at a summer camp for the Norweigan Labour Party and 8 people in the government quarter of Oslo), was described in a *Telegraph* headline as a 'quiet and modest man',[33] and the *Daily*

---

31   www.latimes.com/nation/la-na-charleston-lone-wolf-20150620-story.html (last accessed 08/2020).

32   www.washingtonpost.com/blogs/post-partisan/wp/2015/06/19/dylann-roof-white-supremacist-lone-wolf/ (last accessed 08/2020).

33   www.telegraph.co.uk/news/worldnews/europe/norway/8657066/Norway-killings-the-quiet-and-modest-man-who-became-peacetime-Europes-worst-mass-killer.html (last accessed 08/2020).

Mirror reported that the Christchurch terrorist Brenton Tarrant had been an 'angelic boy'. Considering that terror attacks by people identified as Muslim receive 357 per cent more media attention than attacks by non-Muslims,[34] it is evident that we are dealing with a two-tier system of media representation. One tier (for white citizens) is nuanced, compassionate, willing to look beyond the facts to present context and name complications, and the lower tier (for everybody else) is heavy-handed and cheap, reverting to easy stereotypes which whip up scandal and outcry, and plug directly into political agendas.

It is clear, then, that media narratives both respond to and fuel public opinion and behaviours as well as state-level decision-making around borders. The announcement by David Cameron on 20 February 2016 that the EU referendum would be held in June was the intended conclusion of years of anti-migrant messaging churned out as UKIP ascended to its peak. The vote in June 2016 returned a pretty indecisive result: 48.1 per cent voted to remain in the EU and 51.9 per cent voted to leave. However, the toxic debate which coalesced around the referendum transformed this moment into a proxy vote on the heart and soul of Britain. A poll by Ipsos MORI revealed that for a third of people, 'the number of immigrants coming into Britain' was the main issue guiding their vote in the referendum.[35]

Unpacking 'border anxiety'

The impacts of these narratives are huge. Brexit and its surrounding 'debates' – over a decade of specific and targeted anti-migrant

---

34   www.theguardian.com/us-news/2018/jul/20/muslim-terror-attacks-press-coverage-study (last accessed 08/2020).

35   www.ipsos.com/ipsos-mori/en-uk/immigration-now-top-issue-voters-eu-referendum (last accessed 08/2020).

rhetoric and attacks – has led the two-headed cerberus of Britain's political elite and news media industry charging down a path of draconian and exclusionary Immigration Acts, plans to end freedom of movement and the chipping away of the welfare state – all of which we will explore in more detail in the following chapter. The collateral has been significant: during the EU referendum campaign the political assassination of Labour MP Jo Cox by far-right extremist, Thomas Mair, happened because Cox was a passionate and dedicated advocate supporter of migrants' rights. It is crucial to also acknowledge that Jo Cox was murdered because she was a woman; as Janey Stephenson writes for the *Independent*: 'Toxic masculinity is what entitles a man to take a weapon and take other people's lives in the name of his values.' The unifying detail among terrorist attacks in Britain (and globally) is that they are overwhelmingly carried out by men.

It seems that the more politicians talk about borders and migration, whatever the message (and in the UK media, often the message is sensationalised, individualised, or hostile to migrant communities), the public is left with a sense that the borders are vulnerable. A 2019 UK study supports this idea of a relationship between repeated messages about immigration and what the researchers describe as 'border anxiety': a low level of confidence in the security of Britain's border.[36] Professor Bastian A. Vollmer explains the paradox that emerges here, noting that 'Borders are open but secure – a difficult message to bring across an audience that is struggling with an environment increasingly dictated by confusion and ambiguity.'[37] This message is especially difficult to convey if the media industry doing the conveying is far removed from the realities of the border regime.

---

36   www.sciencedirect.com/science/article/pii/S0962629818301963 (last accessed 08/2020).
37   Ibid.

Borders have their foundations in centuries-old racist tropes. In the present day, the concerted dehumanisation of people who cross borders, by politicians competing to swing further to the right, dovetails with global attacks on working-class solidarity. In this context, media narratives tell incomplete stories, reducing the 'hot and cold' approach Britain takes to inviting labour (almost in the abstract) to its shores while making life for working-class migrant communities untenable, to individual instances of border-crossing and border violence. The inconsistency here is irreconcilable: Britain's most consistent export is its own inflated sense of its own greatness, and yet outrage is meted out on anyone who wishes to cross its borders and venture in.

Chapter 5

Everyday borders and *de facto* border guards

'To me, the word "hostile" just sounds negative. If someone says that we have created a hostile environment, the word is just a very negative word. It is quite un-British to use with people.' – Sajid Javid, UK Home Secretary

'As a migrant woman, we feel scared. If I go [to organisations or social services] they will ask whether I am here legally or illegally, I'm here illegally, so maybe they are going to call the police, they are going to try to deport me.' – Samira, interviewed by the Step Up Migrant Women campaign

Borders can be many things at the same time: restrictive and aspirational, 'open but secure', and destructive as well as generative. Borders are loaded with so much meaning because, beyond the practical components of barbed wire, fencing, bricks and checkpoints; they exist within minds and attitudes. They also tell stories about power and freedom. When we experience a border, it asks us questions: where are you really from? How long will you stay? How much money do you have? Who will you bring with you? The answers to these questions either provide keys to unlock the border fortress, or provoke more puzzles to decode and barriers to vault over.

Borders are not simply policed and enforced at the point of entry – for example, at an airport or seaport, where you might present a visa, answer questions about the length of your visit, or claim asylum. Britain's borders, in particular, have been increasingly enforced over the past decade from *within* the country. In Britain we are living – or attempting to live, in defiance of the laws and policies which are stacked against us – in a 'hostile environment' of everyday borders. The hostile environment is not just a buzzword. It is a living and breathing ecosystem which pulls together the most violent agents of the state, such as the police and border force, and pours profit into private industries which benefit from curtailing the flourishing of our communities and the movement of people.

Borders, borders, everywhere

Border enforcement takes many forms; sometimes walls and fences are constructed through words and incremental shifts in positions and policies. In May 2012, Theresa May (then Britain's Home Secretary, later Prime Minister) declared that 'The aim is to create here in Britain a really hostile environment for illegal migration.'[1] The 'hostile environment' signals the ramping up and codifying into policy of an approach that has been quietly developing for decades: an eternally conflicting approach to immigration that (sometimes) welcomes migrant labour, but doesn't want those same communities to put down roots, live comfortable lives and 'become British'. For example: when the

---

1   www.telegraph.co.uk/news/uknews/immigration/9291483/Theresa-May-interview-Were-going-to-give-illegal-migrants-a-really-hostile-reception.html (last accessed 08/2020).

Windrush docked in Essex after its passengers were 'invited' to rebuild Britain, government ministers reassured themselves that people from the sunny climes of Jamaica wouldn't 'last one winter in England'.[2]

Throughout history, efforts have been made to prevent the growth of migrant communities through stopping them having families and children on British soil. As is often the case with the narratives of marginalised people, many of these histories are hidden in plain sight. Marie Stopes, who founded the first birth control clinic in Britain in 1921 and is broadly celebrated as a feminist icon, was a firm proponent of eugenics and reportedly sent a book of love poems to Adolf Hitler. Stopes' 1920 book *Radiant Motherhood* advocated for the passage of legislation 'to ensure the sterility of the hopelessly rotten and racially diseased', and her founding of the Society for Constructive Birth Control and Racial Progress provided the basis for her clinics. A few decades later, the long-lasting contraceptive Depo-Provera, which has numerous negative side-effects and can result in long periods of sterility, was used in the 1970s and 1980s by colonial governments in Zimbabwe and South Africa, as well as in the US and the UK to 'control' black and low-income populations, and was in many cases administered without informed consent.[3]

Fast forward to the present day, and governments globally are still attempting to sterilise migrant communities. In 2018 Victoria Basma writes for *gal-dem* that Ethiopians in Israel have reported being 'forced or coerced into receiving inoculations, which in fact turned out to be the long-lasting contraceptive

2   D. Olusoga, *Black and British: A Forgotten History* (London: Pan Books, 2016).

3   J. Scully, 'Black Women and the Development of International Reproductive Health Norms,' in J. Levitt (ed.), *Black Women and International Law: Deliberate Interactions, Movements and Actions* (Cambridge, UK: Cambridge University Press, 2015).

drug Depo-Provera'.[4] The unspoken sentiment underpinning such abusive practices is that states often desire low-paid migrant labour, but want to prevent migrant communities from develping a sense of belonging.

Scapegoating whole communities

One month after Theresa May announced the hostile environment approach, the Labour party threw their hat in the ring, with then party leader Ed Miliband giving a speech where he said that 'Worrying about immigration, talking about immigration, thinking about immigration, does not make [people] bigots.'[5] This aphorism doesn't quite ring true: in the context of a sociopolitical climate where migrant communities are being blamed for an economic recession which has nothing to do with us, and everything to do with the dodgy dealings of the financial sector, 'worrying' about immigration takes on new meaning. Validating ambiguous 'worries' about immigration has the result of feeding xenophobic narratives. However, 'worries' about the lack of government funding dedicated to affordable housing, welfare support, and health and social care, for example, were and continue to be incredibly pertinent in discussions about what communities need to live comfortably with and alongside each other. These details are rarely foregrounded by politicians in discussions about migration. It's seemingly preferable to scapegoat a whole community than to admit your failings or direct resources towards communities that aren't crucial for your government's vision of Britain.

---

4   https://gal-dem.com/israel-treatment-ethiopia-migrants-sterilisation/ (last accessed 08/2020)

5   www.politics.co.uk/comment-analysis/2012/06/22/ed-miliband-s-immigration-speech-in-full (last accessed 08/2020).

By the Conservative party conference in October 2012, May had polished and set in stone her messaging on the 'hostile environment' without having to say the phrase itself. In her speech to conference, she reinforced her concerns about 'uncontrolled mass immigration' and what she described as its potential to 'undercut local wages' and 'undermine social cohesion'[6] – the primary example of which seemed to be a concern about primary school children speaking English as a second language. However, it is evident that migration doesn't inherently damage worker's rights, but immigration laws and the devaluation of migrant worker's labour do. As Minnie Rahman writes for *Huck* in 2019:

> Research from Migration Observatory highlights that the people most at risk of having their wages lowered by migration are other migrants [. . .] The UK has one of the most 'flexible' labour markets in the EU but also has one of the weakest labour law enforcement structures which means abusive employers are able to get away with the exploitation of workers. In many cases, migrant workers are actually leading the battle to ensure that standards rise for all workers.[7]

Despite trade union membership being generally lower among migrant populations in comparison to British-born workers (by around 25 per cent),[8] migrant workers are over-represented in precarious industries and as Rahman notes, are often at the forefront of pushes for better working conditions due to the

6 www.politics.co.uk/comment-analysis/2012/10/09/theresa-may-speech-in-full (last accessed 08/2020).

7 www.huckmag.com/perspectives/opinion-perspectives/labour-cant-back-down-on-freedom-of-movement/ (last accessed 08/2020).

8 https://ukdataservice.ac.uk/media/604986/davies.pdf (last accessed 08/2020).

exploitation they face. Trade unions such as the Independent Workers' Union of Great Britain (IWGB) and United Voices of the World (UVW) are led largely by migrant worker members in precarious industries such as security, cleaning and private hire driving. In 2013 the IWGB's Tres Cosas ('three things') campaign led by cleaners at the University of London won sick pay, holiday pay and pensions from their employer, after a long battle. Throughout 2019, Deliveroo couriers held a series of spontaneous wildcat strikes and blockades of catering units,[9] alongside Uber drivers from the United Private Hire Drivers (UPHD) branch of the IWGB, all demanding fair pay and an end to unfair dismissals.[10] These hard-fought campaigns illustrate that far from 'undercutting local wages', migrant workers are in fact fighting to raise working conditions for all of us.

Alongside fighting for basic rights and protections, another barrier which migrant communities have to navigate to access work, are 'right to work' checks, which have made employers responsible for checking their employees' immigration status. Right to work checks were brought in under the Immigration, Asylum and Nationality Act 2006, as part of a government crackdown on 'illegal working'. Employers now face a potential £20,000 fine per worker for employing someone who cannot prove their right to live and work in the UK. Under the hostile environment, this turns employers into border guards who are encouraged to collaborate with immigration enforcement to enact raids, and facilitate detention and deportation of workers. In July 2016, burger restaurant chain Byron called workers into meetings at a dozen of its branches under the guise

9   https://notesfrombelow.org/article/deliveroo-workers-launch-new-strike-wave (last accessed 08/2020).
10   Uber drivers earn an average hourly wage of £5 and must work up to 30 hours a week before breaking even.

of learning about new recipes and food safety. Within minutes of staff arriving, immigration officers burst into the restaurants, equipped with lists of names and photos, which workers suspect had been provided by Byron's head office.[11] 35 people were detained, at least 25 of whom were deported,[12] sparking protests against the chain. Labour market discrimination is largely encouraged by immigration laws which make employing migrant workers appear risky and undesirable. As a result of this, as well as lack of recognition of overseas qualifications, migrant workers are more likely to work night shifts and in non-permanent and precarious jobs.[13]

Being 'tough on immigration' to win votes

Knowing that migrant communities are spearheading campaigns to improve conditions for all working-class people, attempts to separate out migrant communities from other workers are thinly veiled racist strategies which prevent bosses being held accountable for dodgy practices. In his 2012 speech, Labour leader Ed Miliband said that the party had become 'too disconnected from the concerns of working people'. Underpinning Miliband's claim was a call to recognise the 'costs' of immigration – a narrative which both Labour and the Conservatives would continue to run with, despite the widely acknowledged fact that migrant communities make a larger net contribution (of £2.3k) to the British economy than British citizens do.[14]

---

11   www.theguardian.com/uk-news/2016/jul/28/it-was-a-fake-meeting-byron-hamburgers-staff-on-immigration-raid (last accessed 08/2020).

12   Ibid.

13   https://migrationobservatory.ox.ac.uk/resources/briefings/migrants-in-the-uk-labour-market-an-overview/ (last accessed 08/2020).

14   www.globalcitizen.org/en/content/how-much-do-eu-migrant-workers-contribute-to-uk/ (last accessed 08/2020).

The suggestion that Labour is 'disconnected' from the 'working people' also formed a key part of the rhetoric across the political spectrum in discussions following the December 2019 election, when the Conservative party won with 43.6 per cent of the vote. The idea of being 'soft' on immigration in 2012, or championing free movement in 2019 were retrospectively framed as Labour party tactics that had alienated the 'working class'. However, this logic doesn't stack up. When Labour MP Jess Phillips wrote in the *Guardian* in the wake of the 2019 election that the party needed to 'reconnect with those working-class voters', presumably she didn't mean the working-class people living in 61 of the 63 most diverse constituencies who *had* voted Labour.[15] Seemingly, what was meant by the 'working class' in these cases were voters who were willing to reinforce borders at any cost.

Human rights organisation Liberty has referred to the hostile environment approach enshrined in the Immigration Act as 'policy of forced destitution [. . .] [which] as a tool of immigration control – for those who may already be highly vulnerable and facing exploitation – has obvious grave and ethical implications for our society'.[16] This forced destitution hits marginalised migrant women and women of colour the hardest, as they are more likely to use (and therefore be affected by the absence of) public services, more likely to make up for lost services through unpaid care work, and are directly affected by disproportionate cuts to specialist support services during the current period of austerity.[17] Theresa May's portfolio of anti-migrant policies – a relentless xenophobic campaign which enshrined a tranche

---

15 https://twitter.com/omaromalleykhan/status/1205422430346498048 (last accessed 08/2020).

16 https://publications.parliament.uk/pa/ld201314/ldhansrd/text/140210-0002.htm (last accessed 08/2020).

17 https://novaramedia.com/2017/10/02/bme-womens-refuges-in-london-have-lost-half-their-annual-council-funding-since-2009/ (last accessed 08/2020).

of racist policies into UK law – comprises her legacy as prime minister. Despite famously wearing a T-shirt in 2006 which bore the slogan 'this is what a feminist looks like', Theresa May has consistently enacted policies which directly target migrant women and women of colour.

Transforming everyday people into border guards

One of the next milestone moments in the development of May's hostile environment happened in 2013. The Home Office sent vans into six of the most diverse boroughs in London[18] bearing billboards which warned residents to 'go home or face arrest', and included a number to text for free advice on obtaining travel documents. The vans were met with incredibly negative public backlash, and the Home Office was criticised for adopting the 1970s rhetoric of the National Front, a racist, fascist and neo-Nazi party whose supporters used the slogan 'go home' in their racist graffiti in decades gone. As Channel 4 presenter Krishnan Guru-Murthy remarked at the time: 'Anyone, any immigrant or non-white person who grew up in the '60s, '70s and '80s heard that phrase as a term of racist abuse – and the government has put it on a poster.' The campaign was binned after one month, during which time – according to a Home Office evaluation – 1,561 texts had been sent to the advice line, 1,034 of which were hoax messages. When criticised in the House of Commons, Theresa May said that 'some returns were achieved' with the vans, but that they had been 'too blunt an instrument'.[19]

18 https://data.london.gov.uk/dataset/ethnic-groups-borough (last accessed 08/2020).

19 https://publications.parliament.uk/pa/cm201314/cmhansrd/cm131022/debtext/131022-0001.htm (last accessed 08/2020).

The year following the 'go home vans', the 2014 Immigration Act which enshrined the hostile environment concept in UK law came into force. Timing is everything here; as John Harris writes for the *Guardian* in 2018:

It was no coincidence that the Immigration Act – which enacted many of the 'hostile environment' measures now back in the news – was passed into law in 2014. This was the year of Ukip insurgent and triumphant [. . .] Meanwhile, [David] Cameron carried on making the absurd promise that he could somehow reduce net immigration to the tens of thousands. The futile stupidity of that pledge fed into policy that was less about practical outcomes than ministers being seen to take hardline positions, so that the threat led by Farage would somehow recede.[20]

However, the performative policy of the 2014 Immigration Act had, and continues to have real-life consequences for people in the UK. The transformation of everyday people from all professions and walks of life into *de facto* border guards via the Act is arguably one of the most pernicious modes of state surveillance this country has ever experienced. In summary, the Act puts legal duties on landlords, bank managers, doctors, members of the clergy and more to check our immigration status and if they see fit, deny access to services. The Act also gives immigration officers more powers to use 'reasonable force where necessary', meaning that immigration checks are now backed up by the threat of violence.

Data collection on the nationality and country of birth of school children was also initiated through the school census.

---

20 www.theguardian.com/commentisfree/2018/apr/23/ukip-collapsed-online-activism-immigration (last accessed 08/2020).

After a Freedom of Information Act request revealed that the schools data was being shared with the Home Office and police, campaign group Schools ABC led a successful parent boycott of the census, forcing the government to retract these plans. Another attack on migrant school children came in the form of the Prevent strategy, which attempts to identify people who are involved in or at risk of becoming involved in terrorism. The 2015 Counter-Terrorism and Security Act places a duty on teachers in schools, colleges and universities, social workers and nursery nurses to be alert to signs of extremism and refer children to the Channel deradicalisation programme. In reality, Prevent constitutes racial profiling and surveillance of children; the incredibly broad indicators of radicalisation include children 'changing their style of dress or personal appearance to accord with [a new] group', as well as 'having occupational skills that can enable acts of terrorism (such as civil engineering, pharmacology or construction)'. A report by Human Rights Watch concluded that the strategy was 'targeting Muslim children [. . .] and creating a dynamic in which Muslim youth come to be fearful of the educational setting and distrustful of their teachers and their classmates',[21] and risked violating children's fundamental human right to education, freedom of expression and to live free from discrimination.

Another policy in the Immigration Act, dubbed the 'Right to Rent' checks, also sought to block migrant communities from another crucial pillar of society: housing. Right to rent places a duty on landlords, estate agents and people taking in a subletter or lodger to check their immigration status, or risk a fine or jail time. This development was met with alarm from both migrant's rights organisations and the private rental sector; the Joint

---

21 www.statewatch.org/media/documents/news/2016/jul/preventing-education-final-to-print-3.compressed-1.pdf (last accessed 08/2020).

Council for the Welfare of Immigrants (JWCI)'s independent evaluation of the policy revealed that 42 per cent of landlords are now less likely to rent to someone who doesn't have a British passport, and 27 per cent are reluctant to engage with tenants who have 'foreign' accents or names.[22] The lack of clarity within the policy (72 per cent of landlords don't understand what Right to Rent obliges them to do)[23] means that landlords typically act above and beyond what is required, creating more hoops for renters to jump through.

The Park family,[24] who had been renting in the UK since 1997, when they migrated to the UK from South Korea were immediately affected by this policy change. All of the family members have indefinite leave to remain, but none hold British passports. Reflecting on their experience of renting in the wake of the Immigration Act, a family member told me:

> We've never had to give so much information; never had someone badger us so much. We've never had to give so many references; never had to give bank details for each family member. We've never been requested to prove identity with all of our documents as if we're going through Ellis Island or something.

The Park family eventually pulled out of the rental process in order to stop the agent's harassing demands for documents. The family lost their £350 deposit and Mrs Park was hospitalised with a heart complaint, which her doctor stated had been exacerbated by the stress of the Right to Rent checks. Many more

---

22 www.jcwi.org.uk/Handlers/Download.ashx?IDMF=5ab15f33-ae32-4e66-b040-402b71392177 (last accessed 08/2020).

23 Ibid.

24 Names have been changed to protect identity.

individuals and families have been affected in similar ways by Right to Rent, and in March 2019, the High Court ruled that the policy constituted a breach of human rights. This ruling, which prevented further roll out of the process to Scotland, Wales and Northern Ireland, found that Right to Rent was having negligible immigration enforcement impacts, and that any outcomes for the Home Office were vastly overshadowed by its 'discriminatory effect'.

The performance of tackling modern slavery

In contrast, other aspects of the hostile environment are better concealed within less overtly racist packaging, and therefore are much more difficult to challenge. The 2015 Modern Slavery Act, for example, was ushered in as a landmark piece of legislation offering protections for victims of modern slavery and trafficking. The Act promotes some important principles: tackling modern slavery and labour exploitation. However, when taken in tandem with the Immigration Acts of 2014 and 2016, the 2015 Modern Slavery Act becomes another way for exploitation and immigration enforcement to be carried out. As Meri Åhlberg writes on the Focus on Labour Exploitation (FLEX) blog:

Firstly, the Immigration Act 2016 criminalised undocumented work through the 'offence of illegal working'. Rather than preventing undocumented migrants from working, this measure pushes people into informal jobs where they are less protected against abusive employment practices [. . .] hostile environment measures make migrant workers feel they have no rights, and that they will be penalized for speaking up. These are the conditions in which exploitation thrives.[25]

25 www.labourexploitation.org/news/hostile-environment-undermines-uk-government%E2%80%99s-modern-slavery-agenda (last accessed 08/2020).

The narrative spun by the Modern Slavery Act is that villainous lone wolf traffickers and gang-masters are the root cause of modern slavery. Also playing into this narrative are other racist stereotypes about the victims of slavery. Often news coverage in the UK will focus on East Asian women being 'liberated' by militarised police raids on massage parlours and nail bars – in one instance by the very same journalist who had bolstered their portfolio by rightly condemning the deportation of black people.[26] The historical racist trope of East Asian women being meek and submissive subtly attempts to provide a justification for this traumatic process – the idea that East Asian women could have agency and be working in these industries as a strategic choice, potentially as a stepping stone into other work (or not) alongside securing their status, is completely absent from the picture.

A year after the Modern Slavery Act was brought in, Theresa May hailed its success as having delivered 'tough new penalties to put slave masters behind bars where they belong, with life sentences for the worst offenders'. However, as is further discussed in Chapter 6, prisons don't seek to solve social problems at their root. Prisons merely describe the consequences of inequality as 'crime' and lock up individuals who commit these acts. As academic and activist Angela Davis writes: 'prisons do not disappear problems, they disappear human beings. And the practice of disappearing vast numbers of people from poor, immigrant, and racially marginalized communities has literally become big business.'[27] Similarly, academic Beth Richie refers to

26 www.theguardian.com/world/2020/jan/21/what-does-your-10-manicure-really-cost-the-unvarnished-truth-about-nail-bars?CMP=share_btn_tw (last accessed 08/2020).

27 www.colorlines.com/articles/masked-racism-reflections-prison-industrial-complex (last accessed 08/2020).

the connected system of monitoring, tagging, courts, policing, probation and more as the actions of a 'prison nation' – a place where law and order is used as the primary tool of social control.

In the prison nation, border enforcement and law enforcement work together in synchrony, using 'crime' as a reason to detain and deport, and upholding the ever-present threat of immigration enforcement which enables abuse and exploitation. Notably, May also commented that 'modern slavery will never be stopped if our police, borders and immigration agencies work in domestic silos', here exposing the driving purpose behind the Act: to further reinforce borders. The irony of course is that borders themselves create the sites of harm where trafficking and labour exploitation can happen: without strict border regimes there are limited obstacles to 'traffic' people across, and without the threat of handing a worker over to the Home Office, bad bosses wield less power to keep their employees in poor conditions and on low pay.

Modern slavery laws don't protect workers from abuse

A mere three years before the introduction of the Modern Slavery Act, Theresa May brought in 'tied visas' which prevent migrant domestic workers from changing employers once they come to the UK, arguably increasing the opportunity for modern slavery to occur. Limiting the rights and freedoms of workers (for example, to change jobs if they are unhappy with their employer) provides the conditions for exploitation to flourish. Research by Kalayaan, a charity which supports migrant domestic workers, showed that workers who have come to the UK on a tied visa since 2012 are twice as likely to be physically abused by their employer, and three quarters of tied visa workers they spoke to reported not being allowed to leave the house where they worked, unless they were supervised.[28]

Survivors of abuse with insecure immigration status face barriers to accessing support, as they are scrutinised by state bodies on the basis of their immigration status, before and sometimes entirely in lieu of any consideration for their needs and experiences as survivors. A Freedom of Information Act request exposed that over 50 per cent of police forces in the UK report that they share survivors' immigration details with the Home Office.[29] Extensive research conducted by the Step Up Migrant Women campaign also revealed that two thirds of migrant women feel that they will not be supported at all in dealing with their experiences of violence, and more than half felt that they would not be believed by police because of their immigration status, and that the perpetrator would be believed over them.[30] The fear these threats produce is well founded: in November 2017, a pregnant woman reported rape at a police station in East London, and when she arrived at a sexual assault centre she was arrested and questioned over her immigration status.[31]

Migrant sex workers in particular, report that having precarious immigration status, even in countries like New Zealand where sex work is largely decriminalised, means that they cannot confidently report abuse or assaults. Activists and sex workers Juno Mac and Molly Smith note in *Revolting Prostitutes* that clients of migrant sex workers will use the worker's pre-

28   www.kalayaan.org.uk/wp-content/uploads/2014/09/Kalayaan-2nd-Reading-Modern-Slavery-Bill.pdf (last accessed 08/2020).

29   https://assets.publishing.service.gov.uk/government/uploads/system/uploads/attachment_data/file/767721/Appendix_2.pdf (last accessed 08/2020).

30   https://stepupmigrantwomenuk.files.wordpress.com/2019/05/the-right-to-be-believed-full-version-updated.pdf (last accessed 08/2020).

31   www.theguardian.com/lifeandstyle/2017/nov/28/victim-arrested-on-immigration-charges-after-going-to-police (last accessed 08/2020).

carious immigration status to pressure and negotiate, with one worker retelling the threats of a client: 'you don't have a proper visa here and they will say . . . give [clients] a good service and if not, they will tell the police'.[32] In other countries where sex work is illegal or partial decriminalisation approaches are used (such as the 'Nordic model' which criminalises the 'demand' or sale of sex, but in reality has the impact of making sex work more risky and precarious for workers), the law gives police the powers and opportunity to arrest, bully, exploit and harass sex workers. As Mac and Smith write, police being removed as the 'de facto regulators of sex work'[33] through decriminalisation is a positive improvement for sex workers with secure residency status, but many migrant workers are forced to continue battling with another barrage of state violence, in the form of border controls. This means that the web of hostile environment policies, in their dogged pursuit of curtailing immigration have pushed people into situations that are dangerous and harmful. Under the Immigration Act, protecting human rights is discarded in the ahistorical quest to reduce net migration.

Borders set the stage for trafficking

The blanket acceptance of this simplistic rhetoric – of trafficking and modern slavery as a matter of lone wolf gang masters, for which prison is the solution – was particularly notable in the wake of the tragic death of 39 people, whose bodies were found in a lorry container in Essex in October 2019. The 39 people

---

32 www.swarmcollective.org/blog/2019/9/20/nordic-model-in-northern-ireland-a-total-failure-no-decrease-in-sex-work-but-increases-in-violence-and-stigma (last accessed 08/2020).

33 J. Mac and M. Smith, M, *Revolting Prostitutes: The Fight For Sex Workers' Rights* (London and New York: Verso Books, 2018).

found dead in the refrigerated container had travelled from Vietnam on various routes, and media coverage was quick to point fingers and single out the lorry driver as the true villain of the story, with the *Daily Mail* referring to him as a 'death trucker'.[34] There isn't enough information in the public domain to ascertain the lorry driver's intentions, or whether he had plotted to further exploit the 39 people who died. However, while taking someone without documentation across a border in your lorry is against the law, if they are asking you to do so in order to help them, it cannot be truthfully described as an inherently harmful or cruel thing to do. Of course, the 39 did not consent to dying. In reality, the harm emerges because the 39 people were forced to take an irregular route to cross borders – if they had been able to board a plane and arrive in the UK without engaging with smugglers, any potential trafficker would not have had leverage to extort money for the journey, and the 39 wouldn't have had to hide inside a sealed container without enough air to breathe.

For many of the 39, their journeys will have been funded by relatives who pooled resources to help their loved one access new opportunities in England, with the hope of earning a higher wage than they could have back home. Some of the 39 may have been destined to become business owners like Tran Ngoc Truong, who runs a nail bar in East London and helped raise part of the £40,000 fee that his nephew – one of the 39 – paid for his journey.[35] The media coverage failed to humanise the people who died on this journey, beyond printing photos of their faces, and their distraught families. By framing the Essex 39 as helpless victims rather than people who were taking steps to change their

34   www.dailymail.co.uk/news/article-7789281/Lorry-driver-denies-involved-human-trafficking-plot-killed-39-migrants.html (last accessed 08/2020).
35   www.dailymail.co.uk/news/article-7832981/SIMON-PARRY-visits-region-Vietnam-39-migrants-began-journey.html (last accessed 08/2020).

own lives, their agency, hopes, dreams and aspirations became footnotes in a reductive story about villains and victims. This doesn't mean that trafficking is a benign activity, but we could take care to unpick why it happens, what is driving it, and what the specific harms are that can happen within it.

The true costs of migration

As Åhlberg explains, the hostile environment undermines any positive intention of the Modern Slavery Act through making people feel like they have no rights. This feeling is rooted in the reality of not being able to access public services – alongside Right to Rent checks, the Immigration Act 2014 also brought the Immigration Health Surcharge (IHS), a £400 fee which created a 'two-tier' health service. Currently, the IHS must be paid by people who come to the UK from outside of the EEA, on top of their regular taxes which everybody else pays to fund the NHS.[36] The impact of this is that patients who are concerned about the cost of healthcare, and the potential for data to be shared between the NHS and the Home Office are waiting until they are critically ill to visit a doctor or A&E – meaning that easily treated health issues are developing into more complex and dangerous problems. Dr Sonia Adesara, an NHS doctor and member of campaign group Docs not Cops has explained that since the introduction of the IHS, she has increasingly seen patients with complex health conditions, such as a 65-year-old woman with developed syphilis who had been too scared to visit her GP when she first noticed symptoms.

Contrary to Theresa May's rhetoric, then, the 'true cost' of migration is borne by people who migrate. For many people,

---

36   https://fullfact.org/election-2019/nhs-surcharge-tax-contributions/ (last accessed 08/2020).

migration is both risky and expensive. For example, people entering the UK on a Tier 2 Work visa are required to secure a minimum salary of £30,000[37] as well as personal savings. The cost of making an immigration application has increased by around 25 per cent per year over the past few years,[38] and at the time of writing, the fee for applying for indefinite leave to remain is £2,389, meaning the Home Office makes a tidy £2,146 profit on the actual cost of processing the application. Young people who came to the UK as small children and wish to stay in the UK are forced to pay a fee for Limited Leave to Remain plus a health surcharge every 30 months (a cost which has risen by 238 per cent since 2014), as well as paying extortionate international fees to access higher education.[39] According to youth-led campaign group We Belong, the high application cost 'damages mental health, limits life chances, and condemns even the hardest-working families to at least a decade of intense financial strain'. We Belong is calling for a review of the health surcharge, a shorter path to settled status, and an end to the Home Office profiting from Leave to Remain fees.

Britain's border extends across the Channel

Alongside implementing new internal immigration controls through turning everyday people into border guards, the hostile environment approach also encouraged a hardening of Britain's coastal borders. In fact, almost two decades before Theresa May's 'hostile environment' rhetoric began, in 1994

---

37 https://immigrationbarrister.co.uk/what-is-the-tier-2-minimum-salary-require ment/ (last accessed 08/2020).

38 www.freemovement.org.uk/how-expensive-are-uk-immigration-applications-and-is-this-a-problem/ (last accessed 08/2020).

39 www.webelong.org.uk/we-belong-chasing-status (last accessed 08/2020).

Britain's southern border had already been pushed beyond the white cliffs of Dover, across the channel and onto French terrain, demonstrating just how fluid borders can be. A decade later, the 2003 Treaty of Le Touquet, signed between Britain's then prime minister Tony Blair and France's President Jacques Chirac, extended juxtaposed border controls to all ferry ports in Northern France and Belgium. In the first four years of the Treaty, 10,766 people were stopped from entering the UK by the Calais border force, and anyone detained at the point of refusal were held by private security company G4S, a profit-making company we will encounter in the next chapter, which now also detains people in the UK under immigration powers.[40]

The intensified border controls meant that people began congregating at Britain's border, at its new location in Northern France. By June 2015, as racist media coverage intensified in the run-up to the EU referendum, 3,000 people were estimated to be living in 'The Jungle', a refugee camp in the French port city of Calais. Over the course of a few months this number doubled, and by 2016 the number of people living there surpassed 8,000.[41] For many residents, The Jungle was a lifeline, as well as a deeply political site of activity, where borders were (and are) being rejected in direct opposition to the interests of France and Britain. Despite incredibly challenging living conditions, and the French and British authorities trying to make life for refugees as difficult as possible, with French police treating people in the camp with contempt and brutality, it became a place of action for many, where plans to cross to the UK could be maintained and pursued.

40 https://publications.parliament.uk/pa/ld200708/ldselect/ldeucom/60/60weo5.htm (last accessed 08/2020).

41 www.bbc.co.uk/news/world-europe-37773848 (last accessed 08/2020).

Predictably, the increasing amount of people needing to cross didn't inspire the British government to offer support and asylum. Instead, in 2016, construction began on a border wall in Calais, with the aim of stopping people – ostensibly people fleeing violence and seeking asylum – from entering Britain. A month later the French government demolished the camps, evicting 10,000 people and offering minimal support or long-term assistance, including to children and unaccompanied minors. Speaking at the time, Unicef UK's deputy executive director Lily Caprani expressed fears that in the rush to bulldoze the camps, there was a high risk of children 'going missing, falling prey to traffickers and facing the winter without a home.'[42]

When I visited Calais in October 2019 to report on the situation alongside humanitarian organisation Help Refugees, 1,500 people, including around 250 unaccompanied children, were still living in the forests in Northern France in cold, damp and unsanitary conditions. The level of state neglect through inaction was stark: I met a 9-month pregnant woman living with her family in a tent, and saw young children playing football in the mud while waiting to be reunited with relatives in the UK. I also met young men who were carrying nothing more than a small bag or a few possessions. Many of the men didn't have sleeping bags or blankets – we were told that constant police raids mean that people sleeping in the woods often had to abandon their camps at short notice, and that there weren't enough provisions to hand out bedding every single time a raid happened. Everybody in the camp was working hard to stay alive and keep focused on crossing, despite the incessant grey drizzle, damp, cold and thick mud. The hostile environment had created these difficult circumstances: young guys sleeping in dank, wet

---

42   https://www.theguardian.com/world/2016/sep/26/calais-migrant-camp-must-go-by-end-of-year-francois-hollande (last accessed 08/2020).

woods, as they waited to complete journeys or be reunited with family in the UK.

Help Refugees told me that young children they supported were being placed into dangerous situations by the lack of progress on their asylum cases, and the promise of quicker solutions offered by being smuggled across the border. One worker explained:

> Unfortunately the irregular routes are always quicker than the legal ones. We're saying [to children]: 'you can access the French tunnel connection here; you can go across to the UK on a train not under a train [. . .] you don't need to be under a lorry, or under a boat'. But when you're 13, saying you need to wait 9 months is, like, the longest period of time. Or even 6 months; [. . .] unfortunately you say this to children and then they cross with a smuggler in the space of a month. And [we're] like, well, that irregular route is quicker, but far more dangerous, and that has to change.

Fears that child refugees will be left stranded and vulnerable are well-founded. The 2016 Dubs Amendment to the 2016 Immigration Act, sponsored by Lord Alfred Dubs, which committed to bringing 3,500 unaccompanied children to the UK, was abandoned one year in, after bringing only 350 children over.[43] Then immigration minister Robert Goodwill claimed that the government had met the 'intention and spirit' of the Dubs Amendment, but a Court of Appeal hearing ruled that the government's actions were unlawful, however, retained a cap of 480 on the amount of children who would be permitted entry.[44]

---

43   www.bbc.co.uk/news/uk-politics-38919873 (last accessed 08/2020).

44   www.independent.co.uk/news/uk/home-news/dubs-child-refugees-home-office-immigration-home-office-supreme-court-a8566191.html (last accessed 08/2020).

This illustrates how the state will always use legislation to reinforce borders. The state is not invested in taking meaningful steps to unravel its own power; precedent reveals it will only take superficial action which gives the impression or temporary experience of a form of justice without any long-term substance.

The 'hostile environment' policies introduced through the Immigration Acts 2014 and 2016 do not stop people coming to the UK or convince people to leave. Rather, these Acts and the reinforcement of borders in general make life for people already living here more arduous and dangerous, forcing people – our friends, family, neighbours, colleagues – to live increasingly difficult and uncomfortable lives just so the government can appear to be 'tough on immigration'. The introduction of everyday borders seeks to turn people in Britain against each other. It encourages us to see citizenship only as the mark of a person's right to safety, a livelihood, and the ability to 'belong', when in actuality we know that belonging and identity is so much more than rubber stamps on a document (even if obtaining these papers are small wins to celebrate along the way to justice). Everyday borders erode the function of the spaces and services we all have a right to access – from hospitals and nurseries, to schools and universities. Most potently, the hostile environment has the potential to build dividing walls in our minds, obscuring the threads of border-crossing which have always been integral components of the tapestry of Britain's history.

Chapter 6

The violence of detention and deportation

'No one leaves home unless home is the mouth of a shark.'
– Warsan Shire

If you search on Google Maps for directions between West Drayton train station and Harmondsworth Immigration Removal Centre (IRC) and go on street view, you can follow the route of the U3 bus as it twists through residential streets, down quiet leafy roads, and along Hatch Lane. The street view images were clearly shot on a bright sunny day; cars and trucks trundle along the lane and small fluffy clouds are whipped across the sky. You're travelling along an unremarkable two-lane road, surrounded on both sides by open fields; it's really nothing to write home about. But if you look carefully, at the distant edge of the newly shorn field, you will notice pale yellow buildings with a whisker of a grey roof. This innocuous concrete complex is one of the most sinister parts of Britain's border control apparatus: immigration detention. These centres exist, out of sight and out of mind, so that the British government can lock up 25,000 people each year, indefinitely and without trial.

In the UK, people can be taken into detention if they are subject to immigration control and waiting for a decision to be made on their immigration status. As detention is officially an 'administrative' process and not a criminal procedure, people can be detained on the decision of an immigration official, and this decision does not need to be approved by a judge or court. Although detention is framed as administrative, it can hardly be compared to checking boxes on a form. Detention is high-security imprisonment by another name, through which people are taken away from their families and communities, incarcerated without their possessions, locked in their rooms for most of the day,[1] punished for non-compliance with solitary confinement, and forced to subsist on poor quality food and limited healthcare.

Under current immigration law, a person can be detained at any point if they don't have the right to remain in the UK, or if their residency application is pending. However, a person is most likely to be detained on arrival, when seeking asylum, if an asylum claim is refused, or if they are picked up in a raid or spot check by immigration enforcement.[2] In short, this means that the threat of being held and locked up hangs like a dark cloud over people with documents and without, whether they are newly arriving in the UK or have lived and worked here for many decades. The Windrush scandal is a key example of how people who would not consider themselves to be subject to border control can, in a 'hostile environment' climate, shift into the category of being at immediate threat of detention and deportation.

---

1   www.independent.co.uk/news/uk/home-news/home-office-migrants-locked-room-human-right-day-exercise-detention-centres-refugees-brookhouse-a8058486.html (last accessed 08/2020).

2   https://righttoremain.org.uk/toolkit/detention/ (last accessed 08/2020).

A significant amount of people in detention are detained while attending a regular appointment at a Home Office reporting centre,[3] which for some people is one of the conditions attached to their continued residence in the UK. This means that even people who are proactively adhering to immigration policies can be detained without advance notice. Outside of reporting centres, raids and sweeps are often conducted on shops, businesses, and at transport hubs, sometimes in partnership with other state agencies such as transport police.

Detention centres: a wall of silence

Detention centres (officially referred to as 'Immigration Removal Centres' or IRCs since the Nationality, Immigration and Asylum Act 2002) are equivalent to Category B high security prisons. People incarcerated inside IRCs have limited or no access to the internet; smartphones are replaced with basic phones without cameras or internet access, and the centres are often located in remote business parks and industrial sites, making visits from family, friends, and lawyers difficult and costly. Journalists are not allowed to enter detention centres or visit anyone detained inside them. People inside are often only able to share documents with lawyers and advocates using fax machines, which makes preparing asylum claims particularly onerous. The combined impact of these measures means that people in detention have limited access to justice mechanisms and are cut off from the outside world, and people outside are protected from knowing what happens inside. The wall of silence around detention limits public outrage and official scrutiny, meaning that

3   www.theguardian.com/uk-news/2018/oct/11/britains-immigration-detention-how-many-people-are-locked-up (last accessed 08/2020).

people continue to get detained as profits roll in for the private security companies which run them.

Detention centres have existed in the UK in their current format since the 1990s. In 1970, Harmondsworth detention centre (now IRC) was opened specifically to 'process' people from the Commonwealth, after the 1969 Immigration Appeals Act gave the Secretary of State powers to deport people from this collection of countries. While the 1969 Act created an Appeal Tribunal through which deportation could be challenged, the 1971 Immigration Act gave the government powers to detain people for immigration enforcement purposes. Right to Remain's refugee history project also notes that some buildings which had acted as welcome and reception centres to Vietnamese refugees in the 1980s, such as Morton Hall, would later be re-opened as IRCs.[4]

A detailed 2018 report by Corporate Watch which tracks the emergence of immigration policy and enforcement in the UK notes that between 1999 and 2009, Labour governments passed a series of Immigration Acts which grew and galvanised immigration detention and deportation in the UK, while at the same time dismantling asylum rights.[5] The Immigration and Asylum Act 1999, in particular, set in stone the existence and function of immigration detention centres. What is notable during this period is that immigration enforcement went from being little discussed and absent from election pledges, for example, to being a newsworthy topic. Seemingly out of nowhere, close attention began being paid to the category of 'asylum seekers'.

---

4   https://righttoremain.org.uk/wp-content/uploads/2018/09/DetentionHistory. pdf (last accessed 08/2020).

5   These were: the Immigration and Asylum Act 1999; the Nationality, Immigration and Asylum Act 2002; Asylum and Immigration (treatment of claimants) Act 2004; Immigration, Asylum and Nationality Act 2006 and Borders, Citizenship and Immigration Act 2009.

Remote locations and shadowy operations

The UK's immigration detention estate, at the time of writing, comprises seven IRCs (Brook House, Colnbrook, Dungavel, Harmondsworth, Morton Hall, Tinsley House, Yarl's Wood), two Short-term Holding Facilities (Manchester Residential STHF and Larne House), one pre-departure accommodation facility, and 30 holding rooms. Four further detention centres have ceased to operate as immigration detention centres since 2015, including Dover IRC and Haslar IRC in Hampshire, Campsfield House in Oxford, and The Verne IRC in Dorset which has been turned into a prison. The stated aim of immigration detention is to effect 'removals',[6] and to act as a deterrent to people seeking to 'frustrate' immigration policies.[7] According to a senior civil servant, immigration detention is a 'key element in effective enforcement' which 'contributes to the impression potential asylum seekers have of the UK'.[8] In reality, detention does not achieve these aims: the centres' remote locations and shadowy operations which evade journalistic scrutiny means that there is very little public and international awareness of them.

Even the UN's rapporteur on violence against women, Rashida Manjoo, has been blocked from entering Yarl's Wood IRC (a centre which primarily detains women) to investigate allegations of sexual assault.[9] Reports of sexual abuse by guards hit the

6 https://assets.publishing.service.gov.uk/government/uploads/system/uploads/attachment_data/file/728376/Shaw_report_2018_Final_web_accessible.pdf (last accessed 08/2020).

7 https://publications.parliament.uk/pa/cm201719/cmselect/cmhaff/913/913.pdf (last accessed 08/2020).

8 https://corporatewatch.org/deportation-targets-and-the-deterrent-dogma-uk-immigration-enforcement-from-straw-to-may/ (last accessed 08/2020).

9 www.theguardian.com/uk-news/2015/jan/03/yarls-wood-un-special-rapporteur-censure (last accessed 08/2020).

headlines in 2014, when a whistleblower went public with his report that guards used CCTV 'blind spots' as places to assault women, including one woman who had become pregnant after being sexually assaulted by a guard.[10] Similarly, in 2016 attempts were made to deport survivors who came forward in order to cover-up sexual assaults. According to one survivor, guards had coerced women by promising to help them with their asylum cases.[11]

The growth of the detention centre estate has not led to a significant increase in people being forced to leave the UK. In the past decade, the proportion of people who are removed or deported after being detained has nearly halved (from 64 per cent at the start of the decade to 37 per cent in 2019).[12] In spite of the fact that immigration detention is not fulfilling its 'objectives', and despite the closure of multiple IRCs, the British government continues to consistently detain huge numbers of people every year. The argument here is not that detention centres need to be more efficient, but that their actual purpose and function is to merely give the *impression* of heightened border controls, at the expense of the thousands of people who are incarcerated every year – many of whom will be admitted back into the UK.

Locked up with lives on hold

While legally, the government can only detain people who it has a 'realistic prospect' of removing from the UK within a 'reason-

---

10   www.theguardian.com/uk-news/2014/may/24/serco-whistleblower-yarls-wood-pressure-immigration (last accessed 08/2020).

11   www.theguardian.com/uk-news/2013/sep/14/detainees-yarls-wood-sexual-abuse (last accessed 08/2020).

12   www.gov.uk/government/publications/immigration-statistics-year-ending-december-2019/how-many-people-are-detained-or-returned (last accessed 08/2020).

able timescale',[13] in reality, this often isn't the case. People are commonly detained when there is no prospect of their removal: a person who was seeking asylum from Libya who I spoke to in UK immigration detention in 2014 had been detained for many years, despite there being an ongoing civil war in his home country and at the time no functioning airports. In fact, one of the most common experiences of people held in detention centres is that they are asylum seekers fleeing violence, conflict and persecution: in 2018, 51 per cent (12,637) of people held in detention had sought asylum.[14] Considering that only around 5 per cent of people who migrate to the UK are seeking asylum, a minority of whom will be successful in their asylum applications at first decision stage,[15] it is clear that the government is disproportionately locking up and re-traumatising people who have left their homes and communities behind, and survived difficult and dangerous situations to come to the UK.

According to UNHCR, the countries that asylum seekers most commonly came to the UK from in 2018 included Iran, Iraq, Albania, Eritrea and Pakistan,[16] and in 2016 also Afghanistan and Bangladesh. This means that people in immigration detention are overwhelmingly people of colour, and statistically less likely (based on median household income in the countries they have travelled from)[17] to have access to financial resources in order to challenge their detention.

13   https://homeofficemedia.blog.gov.uk/2019/03/21/fact-sheet-detention/ (last accessed 08/2020).

14   https://migrationobservatory.ox.ac.uk/resources/briefings/immigration-detention-in-the-uk/ (last accessed 08/2020).

15   https://commonslibrary.parliament.uk/insights/migration-statistics-how-many-asylum-seekers-and-refugees-are-there-in-the-uk/ (last accessed 08/2020).

16   www.unhcr.org/asylum-in-the-uk.html (last accessed 08/2020).

17   Data collected by Gallup between 2006–12 compared median household income across 131 countries: Iran ($12k), UK ($31.6k), Albania ($7k), Bangladesh ($2.8k).

Targeted systems have also been implemented in Britain to increase the detention rate of people from particular countries. The Detained Fast-Track (DFT) process was in operation between 2003–15 before being ruled unlawful and suspended, after anti-detention charity Detention Action brought a legal challenge. DFT singled out people from a 'white list' or 'suitability list'[18] of designated states comprising the ten central and eastern European countries which joined the EU in 2004, as well as former British colonies such as Jamaica, India and Ghana.[19] Applicants from these countries under DFT had their cases rapidly assessed in a short period (often around two weeks), and 99 per cent of people on DFT had their asylum applications rejected, with thousands of forced removals being swiftly processed.[20] When this abusive practice was suspended, 100 people were released from detention,[21] but for the others who had been removed over the preceding decade, the ruling came too late.

The impact of 'limbo in detention' on mental health

The fact that in Britain, liberty can be so easily deprived in this way is a terrifying prospect. Britain is the only country in Europe where you can be held in detention indefinitely without knowledge of when you will be released, or any limitation on how

---

18   https://detentionaction.org.uk/wp-content/uploads/2018/12/Fast-Track-to-Despair.pdf#page-15 (last accessed 08/2020).

19   https://assets.publishing.service.gov.uk/government/uploads/system/uploads/attachment_data/file/778221/certification-s94-guidance-0219.pdf (last accessed 08/2020).

20   https://detentionaction.org.uk/2017/04/19/return-of-the-fast-track/ (last accessed 08/2020).

21   www.theguardian.com/uk-news/2015/jul/02/asylum-seekers-release-fast-track-detention-ruling (last accessed 08/2020).

long you will be incarcerated.[22] This has a damaging impact on mental health; as Souleymane, a former detainee and member of detention reform group Freed Voices explains:

> Detention is worse than prison because in prison you count your days down and in detention you count your days up . . . and up . . . and up . . . and up [. . .] I saw a lot of people around me collapse mentally. They could not take it anymore – the limbo in detention killed them. I saw people try and hang themselves. I saw people go crazy with fear. I saw a man take a razor blade and slash, slash, slash, he cut his arms. There was blood everywhere.[23]

Self-harm, suicide attempts and death are endemic in immigration detention: while only 0.01 per cent of people die by suicide in the general population,[24] in detention 36 per cent of deaths are self-inflicted.[25] Data collected by monitoring group No Deportations noted 3,581 reported self-harm attempts in UK immigration detention centres since 2007.[26] These figures correlate with high suicide rates: Freedom of Information Act requests reveal that suicide attempts have increased by 22 per cent since 2018, a year in which on average two suicide attempts

---

22 www.aviddetention.org.uk/immigration-detention (last accessed 09/2020).

23 https://detentionaction.org.uk/2016/10/08/indefinite-detention-this-is-happening-on-your-doorstep/ (last accessed 08/2020).

24 www.ons.gov.uk/peoplepopulationandcommunity/birthsdeathsandmarriages/deaths/bulletins/suicidesintheunitedkingdom/2018registrations (last accessed 08/2020).

25 www.medicaljustice.org.uk/wp-content/uploads/2016/09/MJ_death_in_immigration_detention__FINAL_WEB-1.pdf#page=6 (last accessed 08/2020).

26 www.no-deportations.org.uk/Resources/Self-Harm2007-2016.html (last accessed 08/2020).

were made in detention every day.[27] A report by Medical Justice, an organisation which challenges medical mistreatment of people in detention makes it clear that the practice of indefinite detention itself, and the lack of access to justice is the primary cause of the majority of deaths in detention.[28] A culture of disbelieving health complaints, limited access to medication, and the absence of robust mental health support alongside the normalisation of mental health deterioration as a part of detention also contribute to high death rates. In the case of Brian Dalrymple, who was detained on arriving to the UK for a holiday in 2011 and experienced schizophrenia and high blood pressure, staff failed to deliver appropriate care when he displayed increasingly erratic behaviour after refusing medication. At the inquest of Brian's subsequent death while in segregation, officers remarked that they were not concerned about people in Harmondsworth IRC 'muttering to themselves' because 'a lot of people in Harmondsworth did that'.[29]

Within its own policies, the UK government outlines certain categories of people who are at particular risk of harm from being detained.[30] These people include: people living with mental health conditions; suicidal people; survivors of torture and gender-based violence; survivors of trafficking or modern slavery; people with post-traumatic stress disorder (PTSD), pregnant people, physically disabled people, elderly people and transgender people. Rule 35 of the Detention Centre Rules is supposed to act as a mechanism for bringing people from these

---

27   www.theguardian.com/uk-news/2018/oct/11/revealed-two-suicide-attempts-every-day-uk-deportation-detention-centres (last accessed 08/2020).

28   Ibid.

29   Ibid.

30   Rule 35 of the 2001 Detention Centre Rules and 'adults at risk' guidance stipulate that these categories constitute 'people whose health is likely to be injuriously affected by continued detention or any conditions of detention'.

demographics to the attention of those responsible for reviewing detention. However, in practice often people are not 'believed'. In research conducted by Medical Justice, one person in detention remarked that 'The Home Office did not believe [I was a survivor of torture] even though I had scars on my body to prove it'. In another case, a survivor of torture from Sri Lanka had the following comments written on the notes from his asylum interview, after breaking down when explaining that he missed his wife and children: 'loser', 'you idiot' and 'how stupid is this guy?'[31] A widespread culture of disbelief among detention centre staff makes it incredibly difficult for people who are detained to feel able to disclose sensitive information, particularly when it pertains to what might be the most violent and unpleasant experiences of their lives.

A culture of silence

People who have died in detention also include Marcin Gwozdzinski, who took his own life in Harmondsworth in 2017 after being classed 'low risk' and his distress being attributed to toothache; Ahmed Kabia, who died in Morton Hall in 2016 from an undiagnosed blood vessel malformation after experiencing seizures in 2015 which were ignored by healthcare staff (the Home Office tried to speed through his release after learning of his collapse which then led to a fatal haemorrhage) and Christine Chase, a Jamaican national who had been living in the UK for 14 years, who died of a heart attack in Yarl's Wood in 2014. Detention centres often attempt to cover up deaths and keep them quiet, releasing very little information about them into the public domain or to other people inside. One woman I spoke to a

31   www.medicaljustice.org.uk/wp-content/uploads/2016/03/the-second-torture-full-version.pdf#page=94 (last accessed 08/2020).

few weeks after Christine's death in 2014, who was also detained in Yarl's Wood IRC, explained:

> On Friday I saw her talking, but she was ok. [. . .] she went and braided her hair, but in the morning on Sunday they told us that she had died. So then they took away the other lady – her room mate – they told her not to say anything. [. . .] In the church, the pastor said that unfortunately one of your friends has died, and said we will pray for her, and that was it.

This person described a culture of silence in Yarl's Wood, where information about the sinister goings-on in the centre are kept quiet. Yarl's Wood, which at the time of opening in 2001 was the largest immigration detention centre in Europe, has been at the centre of a number of scandals and corroborated allegations of abusive practices. Since it opened, people detained at Yarl's Wood have held a series of hunger strikes in protest of the practice of indefinite detention; in solidarity with other people in Yarl's Wood who have died or become gravely ill, as well as to draw attention to the shockingly poor conditions inside the centres, including inadequate food and healthcare.

In 2002 Yarl's Wood guards' brutal treatment of an elderly detained woman nicknamed 'Mama' by her friends forced other people inside to come to her assistance, out of fear for her safety. This incident led to a fire breaking out, and spreading rapidly due to sprinklers not being installed as a cost-saving exercise, and large portions of the building being made with plasterboard. The fire was attributed in news coverage to protests by people incarcerated, but a newsletter based on reports from people inside notes that the fire was started in a part of the building which people in detention did not have access to.[32] A commonly corroborated detail, however, is that asylum seekers were locked in the building during the fire. In a statement during a trial which sought to prosecute those who had participated in the protest, a worker for the private security company G4S which ran Yarl's Wood at the time said that he had been instructed to 'lock the detainees in the burning building'.[33] Without the actions of other people inside who helped their friends to escape the fire, this instruction could have led to many deaths. A government report states that the fire was so significant that the operation of sifting through rubble in search of bodies which followed the next day (resulting in no bodies or remains being found) was reportedly the 'biggest forensic deconstruction in the world', barring that which happened at the World Trade Centre in New York on 9/11.[34] Incidents such as these are largely swept under the rug; the companies running detention centres continue to operate with impunity.

---

32   https://closecampsfield.files.wordpress.com/2011/03/campsfieldmonitor may2002.pdf (last accessed 08/2020).

33   www.theguardian.com/uk/2003/jul/23/immigration.immigrationandpublic services (last accessed 08/2020).

34   www.ppo.gov.uk/app/uploads/2015/11/special-yarls-wood-fire-021.pdf (last accessed 08/2020).

Chapter 7

Big business and the 'profit motive' for borders

'I can't breathe, I can't breathe.' – Jimmy Mubenga's final words, 2010[1]

All detention centres and short-term holding facilities in the UK, with the exception of Morton Hall, which is run by the government, are run by private security companies: Mitie, GEO Group, G4S and Serco. Running detention centres is a profitable business for many reasons, including the lack of laws regulating them and limited public outrage or concern for the human rights of people detained indefinitely under immigration powers. The companies listed above also run prisons and prison-related services in the UK, as well as globally – which we will discuss below. As well as managing detention centres, G4S also runs the second largest private prison in the world – South Africa's Mangaung Prison – and provided security for the notorious North Dakota Access Pipeline which threatened sacred lands and water supplies. Serco runs eleven immigration detention centres in Australia (one of which made headlines in

---

1   These were Jimmy Mubenga's final words in 2010.

2015, when 900 people inside launched a hunger strike – with some swallowing razor blades and washing powder, and others sewing their lips together) and is currently operating a twelve-year contract to implement part of Obamacare in the US.[2]

Among other workstreams, Mitie takes home a further £500m a year for cleaning and catering contracts across the UK, as well as being two years into a ten-year contract for escorting people to be deported or removed from the UK.[3] GEO Group is one of the largest providers of private prisons in the US. One of its subsidiaries donated $225,000 to US president Donald Trump's ongoing electoral campaigns.[4] For these huge profit-making companies, operating detention centres – places where people are torn away from families and communities and locked up – are just another slice of the pie chart of their business profits.

Extensive research by Corporate Watch has revealed how these private companies compete to secure contracts to run Britain's IRCs by offering the lowest possible price for their services. As private companies receive a fixed sum from the government for each person they detain, any savings on that amount (for example, ways to avoid spending the whole amount on detaining that person) can be pocketed by the business – this is the 'profit motive' for providing cheap, inhumane living conditions for incarcerated people. Low costs and high profits are achieved in different ways, including through paying people in detention a mere £1 an hour (one eighth of the national minimum wage)[5] to cook and clean in the centres. In many cases people end up

2 www.huffpost.com/entry/obama-administration-serco_n_3607068 (last accessed 08/2020).

3 https://news.mitie.com/news/mitie-awarded-contract-with-the-home-office (last accessed 08/2020).

4 www.mcclatchydc.com/news/politics-government/white-house/article136 339433.html (last accessed 08/2020).

5 www.gov.uk/national-minimum-wage-rates (last accessed 08/2020).

performing the same jobs they were detained for doing outside of detention, for an increment of their previous wage, while savings pile up for the government and profits pour in to private companies.

Another way of driving down the cost of detaining people is to offer very little or limited healthcare support or medication to people who are incarcerated – particularly if the required medication is costly. Many people in detention report queuing for a long time to see a health professional, to then be accused of exaggerating or making up their issue, and are often blanketly given basic painkillers.[6] On occasions when people are taken to hospital, often they will be forced to attend their appointment in handcuffs, which can be both uncomfortable and humiliating – sometimes people will avoid hospital appointments because of this.[7] On *Detained Voices*, one person explains the poor healthcare they received in Yarl's Wood:

> My legs [have] been so swollen that I was rushed to Bedford hospital for suspected DVT [Deep Vein Thrombosis], and immediately put on blood-clot-prevention-injection called warfarin, but since then nothing has been done [. . .] my medication[s] have been changed and downgraded because healthcare can't afford them, and the meds given are generic.[8]

Similarly, another woman I spoke to who was detained in Yarl's Wood a few years ago reported staff refusing to take her health condition seriously:

6   https://detainedvoices.com/2017/03/21/if-they-take-me-back-to-ghana-i-will-kill-myself/ (last accessed 08/2020).

7   https://detainedvoices.com/2018/11/11/we-had-no-option-but-to-organise-a-pro-test/ (last accessed 08/2020).

8   https://detainedvoices.com/2018/03/24/to-wonderful-people-on-planet-earth/ (last accessed 08/2020).

> When I told them I was suffering from [high blood pressure] [. . .] they just give me paracetamol, until when I started bleeding out of my nose, that's when they took me to Bedford [hospital]. So from Bedford, that's where they started treating me. They told me I will have to be on medication for the rest of my life.

Substandard food with low nutritional value given to people in detention also contributes to deterioration in peoples' physical and mental health. As one person in detention described on *Detained Voices*: 'The food is tasteless, rice and chicken, potato every week, the chips are cold, the food is totally outrageous, totally s**t, tasteless, doesn't taste of anything.'[9] Another statement says that 'even animals would not like it',[10] and a person detained in Harmondsworth IRC comments that 'The food is very bad. They know the food is not good. Last night they just gave me bread and rice, no sauce, nothing'.[11] Similarly, the 2016 Shaw review into the welfare of vulnerable people in detention noted that food in detention is 'poor', that 'portions were very small' and people inside commented that dishes failed to 'reflect the diets of African people'.[12] This reality appears to disregard the UK's 2001 Detention Centre rules, which stipulate that food in detention must be 'wholesome, nutritious, well prepared and served, reasonably varied, sufficient in quantity and meet all religious, dietary, cultural and medical needs'. However, of course

9 https://detainedvoices.com/2017/01/25/i-want-to-make-sure-i-am-not-going-on-that-plane-these-charter-flights-are-modern-slavery/ (last accessed 08/2020).

10 https://detainedvoices.com/2015/03/13/the-food-they-give-us-even-animals-would-not-like-it/ (last accessed 08/2020).

11 https://detainedvoices.com/2017/03/21/if-they-take-me-back-to-ghana-i-will-kill-myself/ (last accessed 08/2020).

12 www.gov.uk/government/publications/review-into-the-welfare-in-detention-of-vulnerable-persons (last accessed 08/2020).

serving repetitive dishes of low quality, high-carbohydrate food helps the private companies who run detention centres to keep costs low.

Low quality, unvaried food is not only unpleasant to eat, but can impact a person's sense of self. A swathe of research and writing on incarceration has demonstrated that institutions are not just built with the bricks and mortar of prison walls, but constructed through the small, everyday ways in which prisoners' lives are restricted. The connections we make between our food, our bodies, and our identities are at risk of disruption in a setting of incarceration where food is repetitive, tasteless and ethnocentric. As Rebecca Godderis suggests, in her study based on interviews with people in prison: without the ability to make choices about our food, the result can be a sense of alienation from our own bodies.[13] This process of alienation can have the consequence of keeping people compliant, or it can boil over into dissent and protest.

That the British government continues to award contracts to private companies operating in this inhumane way should raise questions, at the very least. In 2013 and 2014, both Serco and G4S were forced to repay over £70m and £109m respectively to the Ministry of Justice, after it came to light that the companies had been over-billing the government for their prisoner electronic tagging services.[14] This practice included charging for tagging over 3,000 people who weren't actually wearing tags – it was discovered that some were dead, and others had been re-detained. Evidently, competence and transparency aren't key specifications when these contracts are awarded. These companies are notorious for engaging in shady and controver-

13   www.jstor.org/stable/41035612?seq=1 (last accessed 08/2020).

14   www.theguardian.com/business/2014/mar/12/g4s-repay-overcharging-tagging-contracts (last accessed 08/2020).

sial business, such as G4S's recently terminated contracts with the Israeli government. Beginning in 2002, G4S worked with the Israel Defence Forces (IDF) to co-manage the Israeli government's occupation of the West Bank and Gaza.[15] In 2006, G4S took charge of checkpoints in an attempt to normalise and depoliticise Israel's control of the movement of Palestinian people, in the same way that the British government uses private security companies (rather than 'prison officers') in an attempt to minimise the sinister optics of detaining people in the UK.

Based on government figures that the daily cost of detaining a person is around £87, a report by human rights organisation Liberty revealed that limiting immigration detention to 28 days would create potential savings of £55–65m a year.[16] As a short-term solution, ending indefinite detention could improve the lives of the 25,000 people who are currently detained each year, but it could also lead to a higher churn of more people being detained for short periods. A lack of political will, despite regular reports criticising IRCs, stands in the way of ending indefinite detention. This status quo works well for private companies who are hoping to expand their detention dealings, not limit the playing field. Academic Christine Bacon suggests that the boom in private immigration detention dovetails neatly with the UK's plans to expand its private prison estate, noting the significance of 'the number of detention places spaces [sic] available [which] began to sharply increase at the same time as private corporations were beginning to win lucrative contracts

15   www.middleeastmonitor.com/20160311-why-the-divestment-of-g4s-from-israel-is-a-big-deal/ (last accessed 08/2020).

16   www.equallyours.org.uk/liberty-report-economic-impacts-of-immigration-detention-reform/ (last accessed 08/2020).

in the prison sector'.[17] The UK now has 14 privately run prisons, all run by G4S, Serco and Sodexo, a company which has a 20 per cent stake in CoreCivic (formerly the Corrections Corporation of America), the second largest private prison and immigration detention provider in the US, which is also responsible for detaining children and families at the US-Mexico border.

No justice in the prison industrial complex

The evident relationship between these different aspects of legal and justice systems have given rise to the prison industrial complex. The prison industrial complex (PIC) describes this interlinked web of institutions and companies which profit from prisons. The approach of prison abolition – which seeks to break down this web by reducing harm and building safe communities in order to end incarceration – recognises that high levels of incarceration don't stop the root causes of many 'crimes', such as poverty and inequality. Almost half of people sent to prison in 2018 were sentenced to six months or less, and at the same time, the use of long sentences over ten years has more than doubled since 2006.[18] This means that huge numbers of people are having their lives thrown into complete disarray in order to serve very short sentences, and that the amount of people being locked away for substantial chunks of their lives is also skyrocketing, while the actual 'offences' aren't increasing in number or severity. The PIC underpins this set of circumstances – creating and growing the motivation to continue locking people up.

17   C. Bacon, *The Evolution Of Immigration Detention In The UK: The Involvement Of Private Prison Companies* (Oxford: University of Oxford, 2005).

18   www.theguardian.com/society/2019/jun/24/england-and-wales-jail-shameful-numbers-of-people-says-report (last accessed 08/2020).

Common perceptions that the US criminal justice system is notoriously unequal and racist (which it is) often overlook the fact that the UK actually imprisons more black people, proportionate to its population, than the US does. Black people make up only 3 per cent of the general population in England and Wales, but 12 per cent of the UK's prison population – whereas black people make up 13 per cent of the general population in the US and 35 per cent of the American prison population. More broadly, over a quarter of adults and half of young people in prison in the UK are people of colour (PoC), despite the fact that this demographic only makes up 13 per cent of people in Britain. The Lammy review into the treatment of PoC in the UK criminal justice system also revealed that the amount of Muslim people in prison has doubled since 2002.[19] These stats paint a picture, similar to immigration detention, in which minoritised and marginalised people are locked up in high numbers, as a 'quick fix' response to acts of survival in the face of poverty and inequality.

Prisons and immigration detention overlap in function, as people who have served prison sentences will sometimes be transferred straight to detention at the end of their sentence, and can be detained in designated 'Foreign National Offender' (FNO) prisons. Such prisons include HMP Huntercombe near Oxfordshire, which according to Conservative MP John Howell, 'has gone down terribly well with the locals, who wanted to see those prisoners transferred back. They can go to say goodbye to them, waving as the coach takes them back to the airport.'[20]

---

19   https://researchbriefings.files.parliament.uk/documents/SN04334/SN04334. pdf (last accessed 08/2020).

20   https://hansard.parliament.uk/Commons/2019-02-19/debates/BA501EB6-8FE1-45B3-B53B-C144D296B3AA/ForeignNationalOffendersPrisonTransfers#contr ibution-F3970DAD-5682-4F76-B168-125A9364E671 (last accessed 08/2020).

Howell refers to the practice of FNO prisons to operate as a holding bay for people who are set to be deported. His comments are particularly callous considering that just three years prior, a young man incarcerated in HMP Huntercombe called Darius Lasinskas had taken his own life after being informed that he was to be deported to Lithuania. Lasinskas' suicide note, which was addressed to a friend who had been supporting him through the process, said that he was fearful of spending three years in a Lithuanian prison, where European human rights watchdogs have reported overcrowding and extreme levels of psychological, physical and sexual abuse.[21]

The deaths of people in UK prisons threatened with deportation like Lasinskas is a growing issue as the hostile environment continues to intensify. A culture of contempt and disbelief by prison guards, as with guards in immigration detention compounds this situation: in one case study examined by the IRR, a prison officer who found 18-year-old Vinith Kannathasan hanged in his cell described him as having a 'smirk' on his face.[22]

Mass deportations and state violence

In recent years, the UK government has made plans to build prisons in former colonies such as Jamaica and Nigeria, in order to further facilitate the transfer of people from the UK into purpose-built institutions outside the country. In a visit to Jamaica in 2015, Prime Minister David Cameron announced plans to spend £25m of aid money on building a prison in Jamaica, where people living in Britain can be sent to serve prison sentences. Similarly, in 2018 Boris Johnson released a

---

21 https://rm.coe.int/168095212f (last accessed 08/2020).

22 https://irr.org.uk/app/uploads/2014/12/UKBP_9_Hidden_despair_FNPs.pdf #page=4 (last accessed 09/2020).

statement outlining that a new agreement between the UK and Nigeria means that 'prisoners serving criminal sentences in Nigeria and the UK can be returned to complete their sentences in their respective countries' and that in support of this, the UK government will be building a 112-bed wing in Kiri Kiri Prison in Lagos.[23] The building of these prisons signals an increase in deportations framed as 'prisoner transfers'; it seems that as the detention estate (potentially) contracts, the prison industrial complex is set to expand.

12,000 people are deported or removed from the UK every year, and a further 20,000 people agree to voluntary return under threat of forced removal.[24] Technically, a 'deportation' happens when the state physically forces a person to leave the UK when they have been convicted of and served a sentence for a criminal offence – this makes up around 18 per cent of people who are physically forced out of the UK. A 'removal', however, is the term for when a person is physically forced to leave the UK simply for not having, or being able to prove, their right to remain.

These terms – 'removal' and 'deportation' are often used interchangeably, but have distinct legal meanings; for the sake of simplicity however I use the word 'deportation' to refer to all forced removals, as the term 'removal' signals an attempt by the government to bureacratise the physicality and violence of this process. Deportations of individuals or small numbers of people commonly happen on commercial planes – meaning that people who are being forcibly removed sit alongside or near to other passengers who are going on holiday, visiting family or travel-

---

23 www.parliament.uk/business/publications/written-questions-answers-statements/written-statement/Commons/2018-03-07/HCWS518/ (last accessed 08/2020).

24 www.gov.uk/government/publications/immigration-statistics-october-to-december-2017/how-many-people-are-detained-or-returned (last accessed 08/2020).

ling for business. Often people who are being deported will be brought onto the plane before commercial passengers board – they might be sat at the back of the aircraft or behind a curtain so as to not 'disrupt' the journeys of other travellers. Sometimes people being deported will be handcuffed, or restrained with straps or a muzzle. They might be accompanied by one or two guards, who are employed by an outsourced private security company: currently, Mitie provides escort services for deportations from the UK.

Deportations are violent and degrading processes: in 1993 Joy Gardner was killed when three special branch officers, two police officers and an immigration official raided her home in London with orders to detain and deport Gardner and her 5-year-old son. The three officers handcuffed her, bound her with straps, and wrapped almost four metres of tape around her head. Gardner lost consciousness and died of asphyxia, and the three officers tried for manslaughter were acquitted. A high profile case of a fatal deportation also happened in October 2010, when father of five Jimmy Mubenga was killed by G4S guards on a British Airways flight bound for Angola from Heathrow airport. Mubenga was handcuffed and heavily restrained by three guards, and passengers later stated that he had been saying 'I can't breathe, I can't breathe' for ten minutes before he lost consciousness.

One passenger remembered Mubenga saying 'they're going to kill me'. They also remarked that three security guards had been holding Mubenga down in his seat for 45 minutes; the manslaughter trial heard that his head had been pushed down between his knees in a position known to incur a high risk of asphyxia. At a trial in 2014, the judge refused to let the jury hear any of the 76 racist text messages which had been sent between the guards, one of which read: 'Fuck off and go home you free-loading, benefit grabbing, kid producing, violent, non-English speaking cock suckers and take those hairy faced, sandal wearing, bomb making, goat fucking, smelly rag head bastards with you.'[25] The judge stated that the messages bore no relevance to the guard's state of mind when they killed Mubenga. The three guards were cleared of manslaughter, demonstrating how the criminal justice system at all levels enables and colludes with the racist machinations of the border state.

'Mass deportations' are when charter flights are scheduled with the sole purpose of effecting removals. These planes, which normally depart in the middle of the night, away from the potential scrutiny of other passengers, are designed to be filled with people being removed or deported. The majority of these shady, undercover mass deportations are to Nigeria, Ghana, Albania and Pakistan – four countries which previously appeared on the 'white list' of places that the British government routinely deported people to under the old Detained Fast-Track process before it was ruled unlawful.

Mass deportations have also been carried out to Jamaica – in recent history up to 164 members of the Windrush generation are known (and many more likely unreported) to have been detained or deported as part of the British government's soulless pursuit of deportation targets.[26] Home Secretary Amber Rudd was forced to resign in 2018 after it came to light that immigration officers in her department had been encouraged to target what a witness to the Home Affairs Committee termed the 'low-hanging fruit'[27] of Caribbean elders who had the right to

25 www.theguardian.com/uk-news/2014/dec/17/jimmy-mubenga-racist-texts-not-heard-case (last accessed 08/2020).

26 https://assets.publishing.service.gov.uk/government/uploads/system/uploads/attachment_data/file/787133/HASC_Windrush_update_for_Jan19_19.03.19.pdf #page=11 (last accessed 08/2020).

27 www.express.co.uk/news/uk/951314/Windrush-generation-Amber-Rudd-Yvette-Cooper-UK-immigration (last accessed 08/2020).

live in the UK, but might not have had the documentation to prove it. Rudd had stated that her department did not set targets for removal figures, a claim which it later turned out was wilfully misleading. In parliament in April 2018, Shadow Home Secretary Diane Abbott pressed Amber Rudd on this issue, forcing her to concede that 'there are some offices which are working with [targets], unfortunately I was not aware of them and I want to be aware of them'.[28]

Despite not seeming to have a handle on the operations of its own Home Office, the British government spends an astronomical amount of money on removals and deportations, and seats on mass deportation charter flights still have to be paid for even if deportations don't go ahead or they are blocked by last minute legal challenges. Stats compiled by the *Guardian* in 2019 revealed that in a sample three-month period, the Home Office spent a hefty quarter of a million pounds on charter flights which never left the runway.[29] Similarly, a Freedom of Information Act request regarding charter flights scheduled between 2014–19[30] showed that regularly around half of the people booked onto mass deportations are withdrawn from the flight. Like immigration detention, charter flights appear to be both incredibly costly and fail to meet their stated aim of effecting removals. Mass deportations are also unlikely to act as a deterrent, as their operations are kept incredibly quiet.

Deportations to Jamaica were briefly halted when the Windrush scandal was exposed in 2018. However, these depor-

28   https://parliamentlive.tv/event/index/b56ca4ad-dc3a-4f36-addc-91a4891f6680 ?in=10:32:50&out=11:03:28 (last accessed 08/2020).

29   www.theguardian.com/uk-news/2019/jul/30/home-office-spent-268k-on-deportation-flights-that-never-took-off (last accessed 08/2020).

30   www.whatdotheyknow.com/request/571304/response/1368873/attach/ 3/53475percent20Hendry.pdf?cookie_passthrough=1 (last accessed 08/2020).

tations were started again in February 2019, despite widespread concerns that more people were going to have their lives torn apart. Speaking in parliament, David Lammy MP queried this move, remarking: 'How can you be confident that you are not making the same mistakes? [. . .] I ask the home secretary, why is it that, still in this country, black lives matter less?' The first compensation payment to people affected by the Windrush deportations was made in December 2019 – one woman was given £22,264 which she described as 'crumbs' considering that she hadn't been able to work or receive benefits for ten years. The Windrush scandal in particular illustrates how borders create a two-tier social system between migrants and citizens – with those who have secure status (and the 'security' of status is often dependent on wealth and whiteness) afforded access to public services and routes to wealth accumulation which cement their preferential role in society.

The detention of people in what are effectively high security prisons, and subsequent deportation is likely to have the impact of signalling to those outside that people subject to immigration controls are inherently 'criminal', and have 'done something wrong'. For as long as these ideas live and breathe in the public consiousness, profit will continue to roll in for the companies facilitating the abuse of incarceration and deportation through the deprivation of freedom and agency. The way that these acts of state violence are reported on by the media – for example people who have served prison sentences presented as 'deserving' of deportation – perpetuates inequality by suggesting that some people deserve to live in Britain and others do not, and displays a wholesale misunderstanding of the drivers of law-breaking.

Yet my experience is that people in detention are just everyday people trying to get on with their lives, who have been thrown off course by the violence and bureaucracy of border enforcement and immigration policies. The people I met in detention largely did not identify as 'victims' – some as survivors of terrible abuse and violence – but all exercising agency and taking action, often working to be released from detention and to halt their deportations. The conversations I have had with people in detention have been joyful, sorrowful, comical and banal: simply, human conversations with people trapped inside an oppressive system. One man I met made me memorise his cold remedy after I sneezed our way through our conversation, and another guy wanted to expand his English vocabulary and taught me words in Hindi in exchange. These details might seem trivial, but the fences, barbed wire and barred windows obscure the people living inside them in all their nuance and complexity. They attempt to make us forget that Britain locks up our friends, neighbours, colleagues, and loved ones on a huge scale, and sells this incarceration to us as necessary and inevitable.

Chapter 8

Borderlands of resistance

'To survive the Borderlands you must live sin fronteras be a crossroads.' – Gloria Anzaldúa

'Sol, sol, solidarité! Avec, avec, les sans papiers!' – migrant solidarity protest chant

In the face of the extreme violence of borders – this relentless onslaught which pounds like waves – we must fight back, even when it feels like trying to battle the tide. Rejecting borders and the border nation is not a simple act. When people ask me if a borderless world is possible, I answer that many people are *already* rejecting borders, through crossing them and living across them in defiance of state laws and interests. We have to dream bigger and bolder than the narrow confines of Home Office check-boxes, bars and barbed wire. We already have so much to be inspired by, and living evidence that a better world is possible.

To explain why pursuing 'no borders' is the route to survival and justice, I could describe the individual struggles of countless people and communities who are living at the sharp edge of border regimes. From young children suspended in limbo in refugee camps, to families dealing with immense struggle as their constant companion as they are afraid to claim welfare support or interact with state agencies, the border nation wields an everyday violence and restricts our right to live freely. Running as a thread throughout all of these lives is the structural inequality that is baked into the border system and immigration policies. The set of scales which weighs up the value of a human life, and kicks out or pushes down those not deemed crucial to the state's vision for itself. Effective resistance cannot be about simply 'saving' individuals, or trying to improve an inherently violent state, but must also prioritise the urgent need to overturn a system that wishes us dead. As Gary Younge writes for *Red Pepper* in 2018, examining the very question of a world without borders: 'If politics is the art of the possible, then radicalism must be the capacity to imagine new possibilities.'[1] There is scope and energy to imagine a world with no borders, even if, and perhaps precisely because it feels out of reach.

It's crucial to bear in mind that particularly in the context of a hostile environment, legal challenges and policy change are incredibly difficult to enact. We will never convince the government to dismantle its own power, but this doesn't mean it isn't worth attempting to make short-term improvements to the material realities of people crossing borders in the meantime. Equally useful is migrant communities and allies coming together to effect change from the grassroots up: pushing back against state violence, disrupting systems of harm, and replacing them with autonomous communities of care. The call to defund police and abolish prisons, in the wake of Black Lives Matter protests in the summer of 2020 are part of this long-term struggle. We can only destroy the border – both physical

1 www.redpepper.org.uk/dare-to-dream-of-a-world-without-borders/ (last accessed 08/2020).

and mental – by reaching across it in solidarity. Acting in solidarity requires recognising the different amounts of power and privilege we all have in relation to each other. Speaking in a YouTube video, Angela Davies explains the concept of solidarity in relation to joining up struggles between people inside and outside of prison:

> Solidarity has nothing to do with charity, in the conventional sense [. . .] when we speak about solidarity we have a respect for the knowledge that's produced by people behind bars [. . .] [and] a commitment to break down the hierarchies that almost inevitably begin to insert themselves into relationships between people on the outside and people on the inside.[2]

Solidarity in this context means, as far as possible, being led by the needs, skills, knowledge and actions of people directly and most starkly affected by border violence. Angela Davis also spoke in June 2020 about the need to look towards trans and non-binary movement leaders in the pursuit of different ways of resisting and living, remarking that 'this community has taught us how to challenge that which is totally accepted as normal [. . .] if it is possible to challenge the gender binary, then we can certainly effectively resist prisons, and jails and police'. We must take care in our organising to centre and be led by minoritised and marginalised people crossing borders, which includes people who are trans, disabled, neuro-diverse, survivors, sex workers, indigenous and more, as people who are most targeted by the border nation create and hold the necessary knowledge for surviving and fighting back against it.

---

2   www.youtube.com/watch?v=Uib2F4Ri4_I (last accessed 08/2020).

Solidarity means acting in a way that doesn't seek to 'save' more 'deserving' individuals or groups of people, but in a way that has eradication of the inherently unequal border (and the forces that uphold it) as its driving goal. Supporting protests against border violence, and efforts to move and live across borders that are led by migrant communities, including people inside detention are a crucial driving part of this work.

Breaking down borders: Protest and resistance

Protests at Yarl's Wood IRC are relatively frequent, with actions of resistance hitting the headlines every couple of years, including a strike in 2005 over poor healthcare provision. In 2018 over 100 women in Yarl's Wood began the #HungerForFreedom all out strike, refusing to eat or work and calling for an end to indefinite detention and charter flights, improved access to healthcare and an end to the £1 an hour wage for working in detention.[3] In their list of demands, which they published on the *Detained Voices* website, they stated: 'Everyone in detention is unfairly treated, and all we want is a fair process. This is the only option we are left with to express how we feel. We will not eat till we are free'.

Protests were also held by people detained inside Harmondsworth IRC and Campsfield House (Oxford) in 2006 and 2007. The 2006 unrest in Harmondsworth reportedly began after a guard switched off TV news coverage of a damning government report on the centre which had been published that day.[4] The report, which the Chief Inspector of Prisons described as

3   https://detainedvoices.com/2018/02/25/the-strikers-demands/ (last accessed 08/2020).

4   www.meltingpot.org/UK-Riot-in-Harmondsworth-Immigration-Prison-Again. html#.Xph2yNNKhsN (last accessed 08/2020).

'undoubtedly the poorest report we have issued on an IRC', noted that 60 per cent of people inside felt unsafe, and pointed to an endemic issue of 'over-emphasis on physical security and control'.[5] After the TV was switched off, a protest erupted with people in detention reportedly being physically beaten and locked inside as fires broke out. Riot teams were called in as people in detention gathered in the courtyard and used bed sheets to spell out 'SOS' and 'freedom' to media helicopters which had begun to fly overhead. As is common with detention riots, attempts were made to prosecute the protestors for 'violent disorder'; in this case they were acquitted.

Since the mid 00s, detention protests have been numerous but generally smaller, in part attributable to newer detention centres being constructed with much more durable and solid components. As Corporate Watch notes, resistance has not dissolved, but has developed in new forms:[6] platforms like Detained Voices are used to expose abuse, and hunger strikes are used to draw attention to the inhumane living conditions in the centres and demand an end to the discriminatory asylum system. Often these forms of protest do not garner the same levels of media attention and public interest as a huge blaze might. Resistance will always shape-shift and adapt to realities, and people inside and outside detention continue to act in solidarity with each other. Detention is not a process meted out on lone individuals: one person being threatened with deportation means everyone is at risk.

Reports in other countries of members of the public and workers supporting people to resist their deportation demon-

---

5 www.justiceinspectorates.gov.uk/hmiprisons/wp-content/uploads/sites/4/2014/06/Harmondsworth-2006-report.pdf (last accessed 08/2020).

6 https://corporatewatch.org/the-uk-border-regime-a-brief-history-of-resistance-to-immigration-detention/ (last accessed 08/2020).

strates the vital role that bystanders can play. Over the past few years, passengers on flights in Australia carrying people set to be deported have refused to buckle their seatbelts until the person is taken off the plane. In 2014, eight passengers refused to sit down on an Air China flight until a Chinese asylum seeker was taken off the plane; he later gave a statement that without the protesters' actions he would have been returned to China. Similarly, in 2015 passengers on a Qantas flight created a disturbance in solidarity with a Tamil asylum seeker who was being deported to Sri Lanka where he would have likely faced imprisonment and torture.[7] In Germany, the 'Cockpit' pilot's union has a policy against deporting people who are handcuffed, and encourages its pilots to ensure all passengers are travelling willingly; the International Federation of Air Line Pilots' Associations (IFALPA) also regards willingness to travel as a condition for transporting people. Because of this, pilots in Germany are increasingly refusing to be complicit in deportations, with 75 deportations cancelled for this reason in a three-month period in 2018.[8] These examples show how borders can be broken down by everyday people performing acts of resistance within their workplaces.

Holding the line

Resisting borders is much more than a physical act, although sometimes solidarity does mean laying down our bodies in order to hold the line. In March 2017, 15 members of a campaign to stop the secretive and brutal practice of deporting large groups of

---

7 www.smh.com.au/politics/federal/passengers-removed-from-qantas-flight-following-asylum-seeker-protest-20150202-133065.html (last accessed 08/2020).
8 www.infomigrants.net/en/post/9461/one-in-two-deportations-not-carried-out (last accessed 08/2020).

people using charter flights prevented a mass deportation from taking off at London's Stansted airport. The group – dubbed the Stansted 15 – locked themselves around the landing gear at the front of the plane, erected a tripod made from scaffold poles, and laid out banners bearing the slogans: 'no one is illegal' and 'mass deportations kill'. 60 people were due to be deported on the Titan Airways charter flight to Ghana, Nigeria and Sierra Leone, and some of them were survivors of trafficking and gender-based violence. Due to the Stansted 15 blocking the deportation, eleven of the people who were on the plane now live in the UK, one of whom was able to be at their child's birth soon after the attempted deportation.[9]

However, despite the Stansted 15's sole motivation being to prevent the harm of deportation, at a trial in December 2018 they were convicted of terrorism-related charges under the 1990 Aviation and Maritime Security Act. This conviction can incur a life sentence. The verdict, which was described at the time by Amnesty International as a 'crushing blow for human rights in the UK' was met with public outrage, and 300 people, including Diane Abbott, Alice Walker and Angela Davis signed an open letter in support of the group who 'took extraordinary and peaceful action in the knowledge that they were saving lives'. At sentencing in February 2019, the judge acknowledged that the Stansted 15 did not have 'grievous intent', and the group were given suspended sentences and community orders. However, the case remains unique in British legal history: terrorism-related charges had never before been brought against non-violent protestors – such is the government's commitment to maintaining border controls, at any cost.

---

9 www.theguardian.com/commentisfree/2018/dec/10/stansted-15-protesters-deportation (last accessed 08/2020).

Borders are also resisted in other ways: grassroots groups like the Anti-Raids Network work in solidarity with people at risk of being swept up in immigration raids. The Anti-Raids Network operates as a non-hierarchical network of autonomous collectives who work in their local areas to enable resistance to immigration raids through sharing information and building solidarity. One of the ways they operate is through their Twitter account (@AntiRaids). Anyone who sees an immigration raid happening can Tweet them, and members of the Network in that area will try and physically go along to support the people being raided. Local groups also set up stalls or go flyering in their areas, with the aim of talking to people at markets or stations about raids and sharing information about resisting raids as safely as possible.

It is commonly reported that immigration officers, like police, use fear and intimidation to get people to cooperate or give their personal information during raids and stops, and officers often fail to tell people that they aren't obliged to answer any questions, and are free to walk away. If you see a raid or are yourself approached by officers, remember that the people being targeted at random don't have to answer questions and can calmly walk away. Home Office guidance for immigration officers states that 'reasonable suspicion' can be aroused by a person demonstrating 'unusual behaviour' such as attempting to 'distance themselves' from the enquiry, and Chapter 31 of the previous UKBA Operational Enforcement Manual included the following as examples of suspicious behaviour: hanging back from ticket barriers, reversing direction or walking away, and 'seeking to limit interaction and/or confrontation with someone perceived to be a threat'. While this chapter was withdrawn in 2016, immigration officers continue to try every trick in the book to make people think that they have to engage and answer questions. Looking uneasy and running away – both valid and understandable reactions to police – can be used against you, so calmly leaving the scene and encouraging others to do so is often the safest course of action.

A government report published in 2019 revealed that immigration raids are increasingly being met with 'disruptions', with one senior manager confessing to staff during an inspection that 'our effectiveness is declining'.[10] The report describes some of these disruptions as 'petty' such as, young people throwing fireworks at an immigration enforcement van, and concludes that the majority of incidents were not coordinated by organisers or activists, but by members of the local community. This is important: 'no borders' politics are not niche or marginal interests, they are lived and breathed by everybody who pursues and defends our ability to move freely.

Finding the weak points in the border

Ultimately, as rigid and insurmountable the border regime may feel and be, weak points do exist as in all fortresses. These points can constitute geographical points of weakness, such as a less surveilled point of entrance or crossing, but considering how militarised the physical UK border is, a multiplicity of tactics is necessary. In Corporate Watch's excellent and comprehensive 2018 book, *The UK Border Regime: A Critical Guide*, different types of border weaknesses are outlined, such as the limits to border staff and resources, limits to Home Office budgets to hire and train staff or build more detention centres, immigration officers' inconsistent lines around adhering to the law – particu-

---

10   https://assets.publishing.service.gov.uk/government/uploads/system/uploads/attachment_data/file/800641/An_inspection_of_the_Home_Office_s_approach_to_Illegal_Working_Published_May_2018.PDF (last accessed 08/2020).

larly when it comes to assaulting people in front of witnesses – and limitations on what injustices the general public is willing to overlook or endorse. These weak points are described as 'openings':

> An opening is a place or time where the regime's control is overcome, or at least substantially weakened. It is still only a limited victory, relatively small or local. But it can become the start of something bigger. Think of a tear in a fabric. Every tear starts as a small hole. It may get quickly patched up and closed. Or it may widen, linking up with other tears, until the whole fabric comes apart.[11]

As we've discovered, these 'small tears' can be stopping a deportation plane or blocking a raid, alongside litigating for a certain policy or aspect of the asylum system to be ruled unlawful and suspended – while still being aware that the state will never dismantle its own border and champion its own non-existence. Every opening expands our mobility and freedom – even if temporarily – and breathes life into the evidenced concept that borders are not inevitable. Each opening confirms that borders are an incredibly recent invention, and their impacts are violent and unnecessary.

A call to action as old as time

'No borders' is also not just about ending physical borders, but it begins with unpicking the internalisation of borders and the social and spiritual divisions that physical borders both create and are created out of. Flowing from capitalism and colonialism,

---

11   https://corporatewatch.org/wp-content/uploads/2018/10/UK_border_regime.pdf (last accessed 08/2020).

borders seek to create categories and hierarchies between people and communities, crushing and destroying our connections to each other and the earth. In this way, the capitalistic pursuit of profit encourages bosses to exploit their workers, and the violence of borders creates the category of 'migrant workers' who have even less recourse to social and legal protections. On a macro level, the pursuit of profit which led to the 2008 financial crash led to public funding budgets being slashed, and the media and political elite using migrant communities as a scapegoat for their own financial mismanagement and self-interested financial decision-making.

By the same token, the demarcation of borders, separating wealth from the sites of wealth creation, has enabled the systematic destruction of the environment. While countries in the Global North such as Britain and Denmark are the top contributors to global temperature increase, countries in sub-Saharan Africa, in particular, are the most dramatically affected by climate change, and least resourced to respond. As the Global North continues to export and outsource production of its goods to the Global South, it also exports its emissions and environmental degradation, meaning that goods and capital can cross borders with ease, while workers are forced to stay put and deal with the damage that has been wreaked on their local environment. If we recognise ourselves as social beings and acknowledge the nourishment that comes from being in relation to each other, this rupture between people and environment galvanised through inequality constitutes deep spiritual damage. The stretching and violent laceration of these relationships is the product of the border nation.

Ultimately, we can resist borders by continuing to take steps to reject them. The call for no borders is not an obscure political concept, but a call-to-action as old as time. For as long as people have been living in the world, we have (to differing degrees of course) enjoyed, benefited from and defended the liberation of movement and the freedom to remain. Border controls themselves are a new, obscure concept. In recent history, no borders is an urgent reality pursued in different ways by a global movement of people. This urgent reality is about creating a deeper sense of personal belonging, enabling more connectivity, and building stronger communities. As Natasha King explains in *Red Pepper*:

> No borders is firstly a practical movement of people taking direct action for free mobility, where the demand for no borders is implied in the action of people attempting to move as if borders didn't exist. From that perspective, the most numerous and active no borders activists are the very people who move without permission. [. . .] no borders is about creating a totally new system, rather than reforming the existing system.[12]

'No borders' is invoked if not in words, then through actions, when crossing the Mediterranean in a boat; when resisting deportation at Heathrow airport; when working undocumented at a restaurant; when a child in Calais attempts to reunify with their parent in Southampton, and when putting down roots in a hostile environment by any means necessary.

'No borders' through decolonisation

The quest to destroy borders necessitates being clear about where borders have come from; illuminating the historical roots of who can be dragged across a border in chains, and

---

12 www.redpepper.org.uk/no-borders-politics-needs-no-defending-its-common-sense/ (last accessed 08/2020).

who can conversely describe their border crossing as 'exploration' and 'discovery' of lands that are already being lived on and cared for. This unpicking involves, without question, engaging in a process of 'decolonisation'. I use this term to describe the active deconstruction of colonialism and its legacy and antecedents (such as capitalism and nationalism), both in the way that states and societies are constructed and governed, and the way that we think about and relate to each other. Decolonisation requires us to begin undoing the harms created through Britain's colonial efforts globally, and rebuilding a new world based upon care and justice. If colonialism involved the imposition of rules, hierarchies and categories, from land borders to the gender binary, where before there were none or less; decoloniality requires the breaking down of borders and these systems of oppression.

Decolonial thinkers[13] identify race, class, and the dual pitfalls and merits of national identity as crucial elements of this struggle, which also fundamentally requires decolonising our minds. In order to truly unravel the damage of colonialism, we must be prepared for a process of flux, reflection and action. As poet and writer Suhaiymah Manzoor-Khan writes, reflecting on the process of co-writing a crowd-sourced decolonised syllabus when her own university course fell short:

Decolonising will first and foremostly not be straightforward. In my opinion it will not ever really 'be' – but that is central to it being a subversive rallying cry. It is a motivation and provocation. It is a word that doesn't quite feel right the first time you say it, a word that should probably never sit right no

13 Such as Frantz Fanon, Gayatri Spivak, Aimé Césaire, Linda Tuhiwai Smith and Ngũgĩ wa Thiong'o among others.

matter how many times you say it . . . Decolonising should
unsettle, provoke, stimulate and dismantle.[14]

Moving across borders and through different languages also
creates new ways of speaking and communicating, which are
real and valid. Chicana feminist Gloria Anzaldúa, writing on
her experience of living at the US-Mexican border explains that:
'Nosotros los Chicanos straddle the borderlands. On one side of
us, we are constantly exposed to the Spanish of the Mexicans, on
the other side we hear the Anglos' incessant clamoring so that
we forget our language.'[15]

Anzaldúa reminds us of the knowledge created in the terrain
of the 'borderland': a space which beyond being a geographical
marker, is a social, cultural and spiritual place where different
ways of being combine and generate new life and ways of living.
In her own writings, Anzaldúa switches between English, Cas-
tillian Spanish, and a North Mexican dialect to Tex-Mex and
Nahuatl, a Uto-Aztecan language spoken in central Mexico. In
refusing to translate into English, she invites us to step into the
rich complexity of living 'sin fronteras', and rejects the flattening
and steamrolling that the domination of settler languages has
performed over the past six centuries.

In his writings, Kenyan novelist Ngũgĩ wa Thiong'o compels
us to 'coldly and consciously look at what imperialism has been
doing to us and to our view of ourselves in the universe'.[16] This
act of scrutiny and undoing also requires decolonising education, family, love and desire, spirituality, our relationship to the

14 https://thebrownhijabi.com/2017/11/01/the-lessons-i-learnt-from-writing-my-
own-decolonised-syllabus/ (last accessed 08/2020).

15 G. Anzaldúa, *Borderlands/La Frontera: The New Mestiza* (San Francisco: Aunt
Lute Books, 2012).

16 N. wa Thiong'o, *Decolonising The Mind: The Politics Of Language In African Literature* (Portsmouth, NH: Heinemann Educational, 1986).

natural world and food, art, medicine, birthing practices and death rituals, economics, leisure, research and knowledge production, work, order and justice, and much more. What happens if we pivot away from the way things are currently done, and attempt to unlearn what have been presented as universal truths and ways of being? This process requires naming 'Western ethnocentrism' or 'Eurocentrism'. This involves recognising that powers in Europe and North America (as settled by European colonisers) have placed themselves at the centre of the universe, while also claiming to *be* the whole universe; ideas and practices originating from these places are imposed as norms and defaults elsewhere.

In the Windrush scandal and beyond, border enforcement has followed and continues to follow policies which are rooted in the same oppressive ideologies which enabled slavery and colonialism to happen in the first place. The ideology goes: only some deserve to enjoy the wealth that Britain has accrued through invading 90 per cent of the world. Everyone else must fend for themselves, earn their citizenship and liberties, or otherwise prove themselves worthy of admission on British soil. This stark injustice has been normalised in the UK over the course of many decades; those who can cross borders with relative ease should realise the privilege held in this action. So many people have died at the hands of British border violence – a violence codified into laws designed by wealthy white politicians who will never know how it feels to have their movement limited. In the pursuit of justice and liberty for all, and particularly for those of us who do not have the wealth to purchase freedom, we can be certain only that borders are not inevitable, and we must break them down.

Conclusion
Living beyond borders

Borders are reliant on individuals and nations understanding themselves to be partially or inherently separate and different to each other. This way of thinking was artificially rendered many centuries ago; the product of centuries of oppression and exploitation. This national and international commitment to borders has been newly stoked in the past few decades, with anti-migrant sentiment whipped up and normalised by media commentators and codified into law by politicians, as globalisation moves capital at greater speeds around the planet, and humans naturally continue to pursue free movement. Migration has always been, and will continue to be a key feature of our society, and people will cross borders first and foremost because they simply want to, and also by virtue of the global social, economic and environmental inequality that capitalism has created – it is too simplistic to suggest that these driving factors are mutually exclusive. Knowing that border-crossing is a joyfully inherent detail of our reality, then, the border nation reveals itself to be the fiction we must call by its name, and resist at all costs.

The pursuit of 'no borders' is sometimes met with disdain and a lack of imagination that such a world exists or could be even worked towards. However, some of the key rebuttals can be responded to. From the borders constructed through news headlines, and the bricks and barbed wire propped up on our shores and in our minds, there is nothing human about division and separation. Every border-crossing weakens the fiction of the regime; above everything we can point to a shared humanity underpinning the urgent call to reach across and connect with each other. I've included below some questions I often find myself faced with:

1. Isn't a world without borders just a utopian, elite, liberal idea?

While borders themselves are a relatively new concept, 'no borders' isn't a brand new idea. As Nathan Smith explains in *Foreign Affairs*, even in the late nineteenth century, most of the world's borders could be freely crossed without a passport.[1] Relaxing borders is not a fantasy idea dreamed up by people who have no understanding of how the world works; we have been crossing, and we will continue to cross. A world without borders is an idea rooted in fairness and social justice rather than structural inequality which is how the world is currently organised. A no borders position does not seek to make the rich richer, or shore up wealth for small pockets of society. No borders requires us to take stock of the harm Britain has caused globally, including to working class citizens and undocumented people in its own country. It also means recognising that the relative affluence and wealth that some people enjoy in the UK might need to be compromised – in order that we can all be free – however, not dipping below levels that the majority of the people in the world would still perceive to be incredibly comfortable.

No borders has the potential to improve the lives of the 50 per cent of the world's population who live on around $5 a day,

---

1   www.foreignaffairs.com/articles/world/2017-02-28/world-without-borders (last accessed 08/2020).

and the 10 per cent who live in extreme poverty, surviving on less than $2 a day.[2] At the same time, a more globally mobile workforce means new skills and perspectives being welcomed into industries that have long been incredibly monocultural.[3] A world without borders does not prioritise one worker over another, but is premised on the idea of cross-border solidarity and building up rights for all.

2. Without borders, how will we keep terrorists and criminals out?

We should ask ourselves: who is seen to be breaking the law, and why? We know that people of colour and migrant communities are disproportionately criminalised, and that law-breaking occurs due to a lack of resources. This suggests that inequality, and the marginalisation and racialisation of people is what creates 'crime'. People are more likely to break the law if their labour market opportunities are limited – for example if a person arrives in Britain, and their qualifications are not recognised in the UK, and they have no recourse to public funds.

Data collected by MI5 on people they identify as 'violent extremists' shows that around half are British-born, and the majority are British nationals.[4] This suggests that border controls bear little weight on whether people are able to commit violent acts of terrorism in the UK. Furthermore, the Office of National Statistics (ONS) data shows that the country has actually experienced a long-term decrease in 'crime' in recent

---

2   https://ourworldindata.org/extreme-poverty (last accessed 08/2020).

3   www.theatlantic.com/business/archive/2015/10/get-rid-borders-completely/409501/ (last accessed 08/2020).

4   www.theguardian.com/uk/2008/aug/20/uksecurity.terrorism1 (last accessed 08/2020).

years alongside a rising migrant population.[5] Contrary to this, a government survey revealed that the public overwhelmingly perceives 'crime' to be on the increase in the UK[6]. Despite perceptions, an increase in immigration has not led to an influx of people seeking to break laws. Increased border controls, and the associated social deprivation this brings, along with the systems of racial discrimination and inequality this entrenches, has the potential to increase criminalisation of certain groups. However, rejecting the border regime is embedded within a politics that also seeks to banish criminalisation through providing sufficient resources, care and support to all.

3. Won't relaxing borders drive down wages and ruin the economy?

Some research has suggested that a more equal allocation of labour through relaxed border controls could potentially end poverty globally.[7] The idea that more open borders and an increased migrant workforce would drive down wages is inaccurate for (at least) three reasons. Firstly: migrant workers and migrant-led trade unions are actually at the forefront of the fight for better working conditions – for everyone. Secondly: migrant workers do not set wage rates (and therefore cannot 'drive' them down), but bosses do. Better regulation of minimum wage conditions and holding unscrupulous bosses to account will ensure more stable pay for all workers. Thirdly: more mobility means

5   www.ons.gov.uk/peoplepopulationandcommunity/crimeandjustice/bulletins/crimeinenglandandwales/yearendingseptember2019 (last accessed 08/2020).

6   www.ons.gov.uk/peoplepopulationandcommunity/crimeandjustice/datasets/crimeinenglandandwalesotherrelatedtables (last accessed 08/2020).

7   www.foreignaffairs.com/articles/world/2017-02-28/world-without-borders (last accessed 08/2020).

that workers are free to come and go, resulting in seasonal or 'cyclical' migration. Workers being able to move back and forth between countries or regions means that they are able to easier maintain connections to loved ones and support networks, creating happier, healthier, better resourced and more stable communities in both the departing and receiving country.

4. What about strain on the NHS?

The current capacity crisis faced by the UK's healthcare system is due to chronic under-funding by the government. The Covid-19 pandemic painfully forced this issue to the forefront of public consciousness; the very politicians and voters who supported further cuts to the NHS came out in the streets to clap for healthcare workers, drowning out the noise of their own hypocrisy with the din of mealy-mouthed gratitude that did nothing to change workers' material circumstances and patients' outcomes. Funding cuts have led to staff shortages, delays in accessing treatment, not enough bed spaces and GP appointments, growing A&E waiting times, and immigration policies which introduced fees for healthcare, cutting migrant communities off from accessing vital services, including maternity services. Meanwhile, the government is plotting to continue selling off sections of the NHS, with a view to privatising the whole service to multinational companies. This needs to urgently change, so that the NHS can remain free and accessible to everyone who needs healthcare. Strain is being placed on the NHS by the government, not by patients.

Relaxing borders would remove these barriers to accessing public services, meaning that people can more easily receive treatment at an earlier stage, rather than accessing a more emergency or complex (and thus costly) treatment once a health condition has worsened. In addition, around 13 per cent of NHS staff are migrant workers,[8] which suggests that enabling people to have the freedom to come to the UK is a vital part of ensuring that public services have the staff and expertise needed to run them. 'Strain' on the NHS is therefore at more risk of being caused by preventing the movement of people across borders.

5. Aren't borders important for protecting the environment?

Borders harm the environment. Border walls and barriers block wildlife migration and damage the natural environment they are erected in, and as John Washington writes in *The Nation*, borders also 'perpetuate and excuse the wasteful and extractive capitalism that underlies so much of climate change'.[9] This means that wealthier countries use the inequality of borders to export the production of goods to the Global South (setting up factories in South Asia, for example), which also relocates the environmental degradation that comes alongside mass goods production away from countries like Britain, leaving workers trying to survive on starvation wages in the Global South to deal with the damage that has been done to their environment.

6. Where will everyone live?

Humans need safety and shelter to survive and thrive, which is why the mythical threat to housing is often leveraged by people who support the border regime – as a way to manipulate

8   https://commonslibrary.parliament.uk/research-briefings/cbp-7783/ (last accessed 08/2020).

9   www.thenation.com/article/archive/open-borders-immigration-asylum-refugees/ (last accessed 08/2020).

our emotional responses to free movement. Yet Britain's urgent housing crisis – which has led to 8.4 million people in Britain living in unaffordable, insecure and otherwise unsuitable homes[10] – has nothing to do with migrant communities and everything to do with the government's failure to provide enough affordable housing. This failure goes back to the 1980s, when Labour councils had built a large amount of social housing and a third of houses were in 'state hands'. Obsessed with the idea of increasing private property, then prime minister Margaret Thatcher's Conservative government decided to introduce a Right to Buy policy, which enabled the government to sell off social housing to tenants at a low rate, putting huge amounts of pressure on the council's remaining housing stock. Only some people could afford to partake in Right to Buy, and those who could not – typically lone parents, people living alone, and low-waged and unemployed people – remained as tenants, and were dealt a 55 per cent hike in rent over the decade that followed. The current government is seeking to extend Right to Buy in England. However, the policy has been abolished in Scotland and Wales.

The increase in Buy to Let landlords (which enables people to buy houses, including through Right to Buy, for the sole purpose of renting them out) has led to a huge inflation in rental prices. The idea of buying up property that you don't even need to live in, when so many struggle for an adequate standard of housing feels egregiously self-interested. People who are renting from the private housing sector in the UK face inflated rents and huge administrative fees, as well as discrimination due to 'Right to Rent' immigration policies, and have little recourse when facing eviction. At the time of writing, in the UK tenants can be kicked out of their houses for no reason, through a 'no-fault' eviction.

---

10   www.bbc.com/news/uk-49787913 (last accessed 08/2020).

The solution to the housing crisis is not to maintain the border regime, as migration has nothing to do with decades of atrocious housing policy. The tragedy of the Grenfell Tower fire – which led to the deaths of over 70 people as a direct result of cheaper, flammable cladding being placed on the building – is only one illustration of how government cost-saving is tantamount to social cleansing. A better system of housing for all will be able to keep step with a more fluid population.

7. Won't relaxing borders encourage smuggling and trafficking?

Borders don't prevent smuggling and trafficking, they both increase it, and enable more exploitation of people seeking to cross borders. As explored earlier, when people can cross borders freely, they don't need to pay smugglers to take them across. Furthermore, with the threat of border enforcement removed, once in Britain, people will be able to more confidently report abuse in general and modern slavery and exploitative bosses in particular, and access their rights and protections as workers irrespective of their immigration status.

8. Britain is full. If too many people come, won't the UK sink into the sea?

On a very practical basis, only 6 per cent of the UK is comprised of towns and cities (including the green spaces within them); 50 per cent is used for agriculture and the remaining 44 per cent is woodland and grassland.[11] What this means is that in theory there is lots of room for more people to come to the UK.

11   http://sro.sussex.ac.uk/id/eprint/54978/1/hard_times_open_borders.pdf #page=3 (last accessed 08/2020).

To borrow a useful analogy from a TedxEastEnd talk given by architect and writer Karl Sharro: the population of the whole world could fit into Texas, in single-storey houses, at the density of New York City. Sharro and many others champion universal freedom of movement, both because it is a route to a world that is just and caring, but also because it is completely feasible. Sharro explains that the solution to real or perceived scarcity of resources is not to pull up the drawbridge, but to open doors. He laments the 'cultural pessimism, this lack of ambition and ability to trust ourselves and our [. . .] resourcefulness'[12] which has led to closed border thinking.

* * *

We have a responsibility to examine where these questions come from, and we have an opportunity to think about what world we want to create together. Getting sucked into misinformation doesn't make us gullible and naive, but it does suggest that there is a vacuum of information and a lack of human compassion and solidarity around migration which has been filled with myths, falsehood and hateful material.

Instead of amplifying concerns that aren't remotely on the horizon, we can take joy and inspiration from the dynamism of border-crossing, developing creative responses to new challenges rather than building fear, hatred, and separation. We can imagine a new way of relating to each other based on sharing resources and caring for our communities. This will be heartful, healing work – acknowledging the great violence that Britain has wreaked and the legacy of these acts that fly forwards into the present. We can do this because we *have* to do it – so many have suffered and many more will die at the whim of border

---

12   www.youtube.com/watch?v=YZZOeroY2_c (last accessed 08/2020).

regimes. By thinking beyond the fabricated limits of the racist state, we can build up from the soil. This involves constructing radically loving ways of living with each other and the earth. Together, we can break down borders.

Thanks to our Patreon Subscribers:

Abdul Alkalimat
Andrew Perry

Who have shown their generosity and
comradeship in difficult times.

Check out the other perks you get by subscribing
to our Patreon – visit patreon.com/plutopress.

Subscriptions start from £3 a month.

The Pluto Press Newsletter

Hello friend of Pluto!

Want to stay on top of the best radical books
we publish?

Then sign up to be the first to hear about our
new books, as well as special events,
podcasts and videos.

You'll also get 50% off your first order with us
when you sign up.

Come and join us!

Go to bit.ly/PlutoNewsletter